Calling the Prairies Home

Origins, Attitudes, Quirks & Curiosities

Mike O'Brien

Foreword by Sharon Butala

RAINCOAST BOOKS

Vancouver

Raincoast Books gratefully acknowledges the ongoing support of the Canada Council for the Arts; the British Columbia Arts Council; and the Government of Canada through the Department of Canadian Heritage Book Publishing Industry Development Program (BPIDP).

First published in 1999
This revised edition published in 2004 by

Raincoast Books
9050 Shaughnessy Street
Vancouver, British Columbia
Canada V6P 6E5
www.raincoast.com

In the United States:
Publishers Group West
1700 Fourth Street
Berkeley, California
USA 94710

National Library of Canada Cataloguing in Publication Data

O'Brien, Michael, 1963–

ISBN 1-55192-680-6

1. Prairie Provinces—social life and customs. 2. Prairie Provinces—humour.
I. Title.
FC3237.027 1999   971.2'03   C98-911175-X
F1071.027 1999

Cover image: *If You're Not From the Prairie* by Henry K. Ripplinger. Original paintings and prints available at Ripplinger Gallery and Picture Framing, 2175 Smith Street, SK, Canada, S4P 2P3. www.henryripplingergallery.com

At Raincoast Books we are committed to protecting the environment and to the responsible use of natural resources. We are acting on this commitment by working with suppliers and printers to phase out our use of paper produced from ancient forests. This book is one step towards that goal. It is printed on 100% ancient-forest-free paper (100% post-consumer recycled), processed chlorine- and acid-free. It is printed with vegetable-based inks. For further information, visit our website at www.raincoast.com. We are working with Markets Initiative (www.oldgrowthfree.com) on this project.

Printed and bound in Canada.

10 9 8 7 6 5 4 3 2 1

*To my father, who was born on the Prairies,
Bob Coulling, who lived here his entire life,
and my mother, who just comes here to reorganize my cupboards.*

Contents

Foreword

What makes Prairie people the way they are? The question itself assumes a difference, that Prairie people, in some ways and at some level, are not like mountain dwellers, or people who live by the ocean, or people of true deserts or of forested areas. This is an assumption I accept, that the landscape in which you dwell influences you in obscure ways to become different than you would be if you lived in another landscape. At the most obvious level, we pretty much agree that lifelong city dwellers are different from people who've spent their lives on farms, ranches, or in some degree of wilderness — if there can be degrees of wilderness. I have spent a long time pondering this question over the past 20 years, and the attempt to frame an answer has taken me through history, geography, archeology, a little anthropology, and, at an amateur's level, even botany and biology.

It seems to me, now that most of the Canadian Great Plains is plowed and under cultivation or grazing, that we have still not learned the best way to live here, for with our occupation has come a changing of the face of the land: grass plowed up and/or grazed, and with this destruction of habitat the destruction of plant and animal biodiversity, as well as, finally, massive rural depopulation. Yet our poets and prose writers still tell of the breathtaking beauty of the prairie, of its magical quality, the way it produces visions and visionaries, of the voices carried on the constant winds, the mirages of the horizon, the northern lights dancing in the sky above it all. In partial answer to the question, I have come to think that more than anything we Prairie people are made what we are by the mystical quality of this landscape: land and sky, and, as I've said elsewhere, what nature leaves out our psyches fill.

And, of course, there is winter, one of the harshest on the inhabitable Earth: howling winds, unbelievable cold, mountains of snow. Winter teaches you who is boss; it teaches you to "hunker in," to set your jaw, to make black jokes, to find a kind of courage for the long haul, and to do the things that must be done no matter what, winter or no winter. Yet winter is long enough here for us to find its own beauty each year — the soft darkness of December as the solar year winds down, the sunny biting cold of January, the rare (and welcome) February chinook, the bluster that hints of new growth in March — but its length and typical harshness also teach us, more than those in more moderate climates, to cherish spring and summer and fall.

But there is also the space that makes us what we are, the very vastness of this place we call home, its blessed emptiness — only 4.5 million people spread out over an area the size of whole countries elsewhere. People who've always had a lot of room don't like to hurry, don't like to be pushed, don't like people standing too close to them.

Those who came here not so very long ago and did not go insane, did not starve to death, did not run away, but stayed to make homes, to find livelihoods, however misguided, that is, our ancestors, are those whom we revere. We feel we cannot fail the intrepid folk whose bones lie buried in our small-town cemeteries and the corners of plowed fields, but whose spirits walk the land in the form of stories we continue to tell in awe and pity — the hardships those newcomers endured to make a place for themselves and future generations here. We know we could never have done it ourselves, although a tiny part of us would like to have had the chance to try.

So: we are tough; we are not always nice, but we'll help you when your car breaks down, or you're lost and have had nothing to eat for hours; we'll pull you out of the ditch you wouldn't be stuck in if you'd known what the Prairies are like; we'll even organize a search party and risk our lives to find you in a blizzard. We may not say much, we don't even expect you to see the soaring, brilliant beauty in which we live, but if you look closely you can read the effects of space and distance in our eyes, and you can feel how silence has settled into our bones and our blood, and you can sense the quiet reverence we share for living here in such beauty. You'll come to marvel at the enduring strength living on the Prairies has taught us.

Sharon Butala

Introduction

Tracy had made the classic, West Coast, rookie mistake. She didn't plug in. A couple of decades living in Vancouver had apparently stripped her of the "winter-smarts" she had gained growing up in Regina. And the result/consequence was sitting in my driveway: over a ton of immobile, American automobile.

"I thought it would be okay for one night," she said, staring at her father's Chevy, white and lifeless.

We've all been there. Some nights, the air is not so cold and the wind is not so bitter and your unplugged vehicle greets you in the morning with a hesitant cough, followed by the happy sound of an engine turning over.

But not on this day.

Tracy was back in Regina to visit her father, who was not well. She was staying with me, because she had brought her infant son, and her dad was a pretty heavy smoker. She had the loan of her father's car during the visit, and on the first night she forgot to plug it in. So there we were, staring at a four-wheeled paperweight, our breath hanging in the winter air like cartoon word balloons. Clearly, we needed a "boost." To compound the problem, the car had died in my driveway, with the front wedged between my garage and my rear fence. All of which meant it would be impossible simply to drive another vehicle up alongside her dad's car. Task 1 was finding someone with a pair of jumper cables. Task 2 was moving the car out into the street so we could get at the battery. Fortunately, my neighbour Frank was home. So was his adult son. And they had the cables. As for task 2 … well, Tracy's dad's car was from that period in the early '80s when it was still okay to build cars that were almost as large as Prince Edward Island. And so it was that Tracy sat in the driver's seat, steering the car as Frank, Jason and I risked communal hernias and pushed the Chevy backwards. The hard part accomplished, we hooked up her battery to Frank's, and performed the vehicular equivalent of cardiopulmonary resuscitation. I thanked Frank. As Tracy and I stepped back toward my house, Frank replied.

"You're welcome. And thanks, Mike, for feeling comfortable enough to come ask me for help."

"What did he thank us for?" Tracy whispered, when we were out of earshot.

"For asking him to help," I answered.

Tracy shook her head with a mixture of wonder and amusement. "Prairie people," she said.

Yep, Prairie people. As much as the unique landscape that stretches across three provinces, it is the people who define "The Prairies." I don't want to suggest there's something here that doesn't exist in such quantity elsewhere. It's more than manners, or even compassion. It's a recognition that we're all in it together. We're all pieces on this sprawling chessboard, ruled by nature and forever destined to be overshadowed by those other, flashier places. And as a result, there seems to be a little more … caring. The nice thing is that we don't hog it all to ourselves. We export it, spread it around. When the sons and daughters of the Prairies move to other provinces and countries, they take that Prairie attitude with them. They spread it around and if we're lucky it grows.

Now, about that chessboard — in the five years since the first edition of *Calling the Prairies Home* was published, I've managed to see more of the land than I had in previous years. More rolling hills, more lakes, more local diners, more northern lights. I've begun to doubt my original assessment that the

Prairies boast a "subtler" beauty than other regions. I remember my first morning waking up in Prince Albert National Park. It was early, and my dog and I awoke to the sound of something big splashing along the shore of Namecus Lake. We poked our heads outside the tent, and traded surprised looks with a moose and her calf. The standoff ended the safest way possible for all concerned; mother and child galloped away down the shoreline. Then I realized we were still not alone. A man at the neighbouring site stood in front of his tent, drinking coffee. "Well," he said, sipping a mouthful. "That was sure a Canadian moment." Yes, and such a Prairie moment too, although many people wouldn't have thought so. We are so much more than combines and wheat fields. Heck, we're even getting into the movie business, with places like Moose Jaw being the setting for both Canadian and American films. (Ironically, the same streetscape that was unchanged by new investment during the Jaw's depressed 1980s is now turning up in American and Canadian movies because it easily doubles for any 1950s small town.)

In fact, with each passing year, that timeworn image of flat farmland seems a bit more out of date. There are many happy stories out here, and some of them found their way into this book. Yet they do not erase the fact that the very industry — no, culture — that built this land is changing. Out here, the decline of the family farm is the biggest story of the past half-century, and the last 10 years have been especially melancholy, because defiance seems to have given way to resignation. Children may not take over from their parents. Farms will grow in size and shrink in number. Of course, this also means there's more reason than ever to recognize the ever-expanding breadth of "Prairie life." We are still farmers, and cowboys and miners, sure. But we can also be Nobel laureates, Pulitzer Prize-winning novelists and dot.com millionaires. Heck, we can even be a couple of shaggy Alberta farm kids who write and record a song that goes to number 1 on the rock charts (see page 149).

Meeting such people was a highlight of writing this book. For this second edition, I updated some facts and figures that time had made incorrect. And I called up people I had interviewed five years ago. Some, sorry to say, are no longer with us. More often than not, though, I was pleasantly surprised. Not only were they still living on the Prairies (the former 98-year-old who was preparing for his 103rd birthday was an unexpected delight), but most were doing well. In chapter 6, you'll meet the Hunter family: five boys who love hockey and a mom and dad who redefine the word "dedication." As you'll read inside, it was never about making it into the big leagues. It was about fun. And yet, on September 20, 2003, the Hunter clan sat in the seats of Calgary's

Saddledome and watched their eldest play his first exhibition NHL game as a member of the Edmonton Oilers.

One thing I want to repeat from my original introduction is the "thank yous." They go out to the same people, for the same reasons: Anthony Cooney, for putting Raincoast Books and me together; friends and authors Kim Westad and Anne Schneider, for their encouragement and advice; Sharon Butala for writing a foreword that exemplifies why she has emerged as the best-known modern chronicler of the Prairies' special magic.

Three years ago, I bought a house. A little Regina bungalow that, like many Saskatchewan homes, can be purchased for barely more than pocket change and a fist full of Canadian Tire money. Maybe it's because land has always been so important in these parts, but that one purchase has, more than anything, made me feel that this is home. As I admitted in the first edition, I'm a West Coast transplant, one who arrived on the Prairies wondering why electric plugs dangled from cars' front grilles, and why the inhabitants talked about the weather with a zeal that suggested they thought they might actually be able to change it (some have tried). Nowadays, it's the practices outside the Prairies that seem foreign to me. Or downright amusing. Watching Vancouver motorists skid and slide their way through a "blizzard" (what we call "a light dusting") is a lesson in how people are shaped by their surroundings.

Chapter 1

Who We Are

SCOTT BONNOR:
SAVED BY A BOOT, A LUNCH, AND SOME FRIENDS

Scott Bonnor admits it. He opted for convenience over safety, and it could have killed him. On August 30, 1998, on one of two adjoining farms he owns near Abernethy, Saskatchewan, he was as busy as one gets when there are some 800 hectares of grain to harvest. As the 44-year-old farmer cleaned out the hopper — the containment bin on the combine — he strayed from his routine of stepping down, walking around the combine, and climbing back up the other side. Instead, Scott stepped directly over the hopper. And, just like in all those farm-safety videos, something went wrong. He slipped. The spinning auger at the bottom of the hopper quickly swallowed his foot to the ankle. The rotating blade would have torn his foot off, but the metal plate of his steel-toed boot came off first and jammed the auger. That wasn't his only bit of luck that day. The accident occurred at 12:19 p.m. Lunchtime. Instead of standing there bleeding and in pain for hours, Scott was discovered within minutes by his wife, Shirley, when she brought him out his lunch. It still took more than two hours before Scott's dad, Charlie, a neighbour, and an ambulance crew were able to free his mangled foot.

Scott was rushed to a hospital in Regina, where he learned the steel toe was the only one he'd lose that day. But, doctors told him, it would be a while before he was up and walking comfortably. He still had 790 hectares of unharvested grain on his own farm and the neighbouring 100-year-old farm he had bought from his father. Farmers don't take days off at harvest, much less lie in bed for a couple of weeks. The solution came from Ray Heil, Scott's neighbour and a retired farmer. "He organized a combine bee," Scott said.

With more than 2,300 cases, Manitoba was the hardest hit in Canada's 1953 polio epidemic.

The next Saturday, one week after the accident, six combines came together on Bonnor's fields. By Sunday, there were 10. Over those two days, Bonnor's neighbours took almost all of his crops off the fields. "They were still combining themselves," Scott said. "But they gave up a day to work on our farm … That took a lot of pressure off."

The neighbours' wives brought food both days and turned the task into an old-time social event. And it was "old-time." Things like this have happened ever since farmers first planted their futures in this vast quilt of land. "It's something money can't buy," Scott said. "It's the people. The generosity of the people. You can't get that just anywhere. We help each other. It was my time to get help."

First, let's define "Prairies." Geographically that's not hard to do. The Rocky Mountains lie on one side, the Canadian Shield on the other, with Precambrian forest and the U.S. border defining the northern and southern limits. And, of course, the area has been pretty neatly carved up into three provinces. This tells us *where* the Prairies are, not *what* they are. There's no one answer. Our 1,963,172 square kilometres comprise one large canvas, a sprawling mural made up of millions of brush strokes. Of all the generalizations one can make about Prairie people, the most accurate is that our feet are solidly on the ground, our heads are squarely on our shoulders, and our hearts are proudly on our sleeves.

The people, like the land itself, are pretty constant. The most unforgiving drought doesn't embitter us. The good times don't make us cocky. Even as Calgary enters another period of growth that threatens to push its population into seven figures before the year 2010, the genuine openness and warmth that greet visitors remain. And always there is that expanse of land beneath us and the bluest sky imaginable overhead. Maybe they keep us humble. The following stories, like Scott Bonnor's tale, should shed some light on who we are.

But First, What We Are Not

Thousands of people call our Prairie tourism offices each year with questions. Many of them obviously learned about the Prairies from Bugs Bunny cartoons. One caller asked a Saskatchewan Tourism official if she had ever really, truly, *personally* seen a Mountie. "People think we're mostly Eskimos in Winnipeg," explained a tourism official there. "They think we have winter all the time."

Here are some of the dumber questions phoned in to our Prairie tourism staff:

- Are there any gas stations along the Yellowhead Highway?
- Are there polar bears in Regina?
- Do we ride around on horses on Calgary's one street?
- Do you have any paved roads in Saskatchewan? (Anyone who lives there could forgive that question.)
- Is Saskatoon open?

A Word about Alberta

BRASH.

Clichés abound, all of them adding up to one unshakeable stereotype: the swaggering rancher with a Stetson bigger than his social conscience. The fact is, not only do most Albertans not mind, but they've also grown fond of that image, even if precious few actually have a ranching background. So what if a rodeo clown is their idea of a performance artist? Credit the ranching and farming heritage for their individualism and work ethic. That swagger probably stems from the fact that no other province enjoys as many hours of sunshine.

3

A Word about Saskatchewan

FLAT.
Like the Sahara Desert, Saskatchewan is known primarily for what isn't there: no mountains, no ocean, no trees. The only thing is, that's flat-out incorrect. The *top half* of the province is covered with trees. And southern horizons are broken by sand dunes, badlands, and the wooded beauty of the Cypress Hills. It doesn't matter, though. The rest of Canada has an unalterable impression of this province. Saskatchewanians can safely admit that the flat part is, if not the only type of landscape, then the most important type. No other province has such an entrenched dependency on the land. The soil is the soul.

A Word about Manitoba

CALM.
As in relaxing and even a bit understated. Manitoba doesn't conjure up an immediate picture in the minds of people who live elsewhere. They've heard of Winnipeg and its famous ballet. Some people remember their Guess Who albums fondly. But what images does the word *Manitoba* inspire? Let's face it, this is the George Harrison of the western provinces. We're talking about perception here. The reality is that Manitoba is a beautiful, bountiful gateway between the west and the rest. It's farmland, mining communities, and cottage country. The lakes and rivers make it an angler's dream. As for your typical Manitoban, well, there's a good chance he or she lives in Winnipeg. More than half the province's residents do.

Are You Prairie?

If you're lucky. There are a few signs that suggest a certain familiarity with the flatlands. One of them is the farmer's tan. Does it end abruptly in a clean circle dissecting your bicep? Do you sit through church fantasizing about the buffet dinner that is mere minutes away? Above all, do you speak the lingo?

"Porch climber" is another name for home brew. A "hay burner" is a horse. Think about it. A "hockey puck" is a frozen horse turd, and it works just as well, although you don't want to play goal. A hailstorm is called a "great white combine" because it mows the crop down with ruinous efficiency. And that sprawling piece of sky up there is the "big blue bin." Above all, we never ever call them sunflower seeds. They're "spits."

My favourite came in a conversation with a Manitoba farmer; it is used to describe any man not blessed with large or even average-sized genitalia: "He isn't going to plow a very deep furrow."

The diverse ethnic origins on the Prairies produced a wide range of languages, but in the home English reigns. According to the 2001 census, it's the language spoken at home by 95 percent of people in the three Prairie provinces. Chinese comes in a very distant second, followed closely by German, French, Cree, Punjabi and Vietnamese.

The West and the Rest

The Prairies have served as the shopping channel for central Canada. Fur, lumber, wheat — whatever central Canadians needed, we supplied. Often at sale prices. And it's hard not to feel that our historical and ongoing contributions to the lives of Canadians have not always been appreciated.

The four-metre-high statue atop Manitoba's legislature is the Golden Boy, by Charles Gardet. The boy's torch symbolizes enterprising Prairie spirit.

How disenfranchised are we politically? Pierre Trudeau's National Energy Policy allowed Ottawa to siphon off a share of Alberta's oil windfall ("One for you, one for me; one for you, two for me; one for you, three for me ..."). Then there are the minor annoyances, such as driving to the nearest polling station after supper to vote only to hear on the car radio that Ontario and Quebec have already determined who will lead the country.

The politics of the Prairies, and the west in general, is that of the outsider. The west has repeatedly endorsed political newcomers, underdogs, and opposition parties. Our Davids have taken the form of the Progressives in the 1920s, the Depression-era Social Credit of Alberta, the Co-operative Commonwealth Federation (better known as the CCF) in the war years, and John Diefenbaker's Tories in the late 1950s. The same phenomenon was evident in the two federal elections of the 1990s as Parliament was reduced to three regional parties. In the west, Preston Manning's Reform Party was elevated to the status of official opposition. When Reform sought its first federal seats, it preached less government and carried the slogan "The West Wants In." That may seem

5

confrontational, but at least we haven't yet said we want *out*. Despite our various beefs, we remain Canadians.

A Calgary-born historian named George Stanley turned a leaf into a national symbol. His entry was chosen as the best out of 2,000 when Lester Pearson's government invited Canadians to design the new flag. Stanley was inspired by the red-and-white commandant's flag that flew at the Royal Military College in Kingston, Ontario, where he was dean of arts. He replaced that flag's crest with the 11-point maple leaf from Canada's coat of arms. The leaf was a controversial choice. For one thing, it made no reference to the nation's historical links to Britain. Pearson dug in his heels, and what would eventually become one of the most distinctive flags in the world was raised for the first time on February 15, 1965.

In times of war, farm kids and small-town boys have always "answered the call," motivated by patriotism, a naive heroism, or an understandable desire to see the world beyond the horizon. Most of the young men who fought with the 46th Canadian Infantry Battalion (South Saskatchewan) during World War I had grown up on the Prairies. The 46th was created in Moose Jaw in 1914 and disbanded in 1919. Between those two dates, 5,374 men served in the battalion, and 4,917 of them were either killed or wounded. They fought in several major European battles, including Vimy Ridge, the Somme, and Passchendaele. Six hundred members of the 46th fought in Passchendaele; by day's end, 403 had been killed or wounded. No wonder these young men referred to themselves as the Suicide Battalion.

For one day during World War II, "Nazis" successfully paraded down the streets of Winnipeg. The city's Victory Committee devised what must have been the most melodramatic wartime spirit booster in the nation when it staged If Day. The event was meant to show what would happen if German soldiers captured Winnipeg. Nazi uniforms were brought in from Hollywood, and 1,000 citizens were assigned the role of the occupying force. As recorded in *Life* magazine, the soldiers goose-stepped through the downtown and arrested the mayor, the lieutenant governor, and the premier.

THE WINNIPEG FILE
In an article in *Harper's Magazine* in 1856, a New York writer described a sorry little village that would eventually become part of

6

Winnipeg as "the end of the world." Today we regard Winnipeg as the gateway to the west and the first chapter in the history book of the Prairies. Located pretty much in the centre of Canada, Winnipeg began as a trading post called Fort Rouge in 1738. Its position at the convergence of the Red and Assiniboine Rivers ensured that it would have a role in the fur trade. While everyone else looked to the west as little more than a shopping aisle, Thomas Douglas, the Earl of Selkirk, believed the region could host and feed settlers. He brought other Scots to the Red River Settlement in 1812, where they encountered one setback after another, from killing cold to crop failure to the Seven Oaks Massacre of 1816.

The colony rebounded and soldiered on around Fort Garry, built by the Hudson's Bay Company in 1821. The settlement became the City of Winnipeg (Cree for "murky water") in 1873. The arrival of the railway in 1881 created a boom in growth and kicked off an era of western boosterism. The Winnipeg Grain Exchange was built in 1887, and Winnipeg became the most important business centre west of Toronto.

Despite the impressive skyline of office towers, the city's financial power has waned. A new side of Winnipeg has emerged, that of a multicultural city with an unusually vibrant arts community, best reflected in the world-class Royal Winnipeg Ballet and the much-loved Winnipeg Folk Festival.

A Common Sort of Radicalism

For an agrarian-based society so willing to abide by the fickleness of nature, the Prairies have proven far less tolerant of the inequities imposed by humans. Few events reveal this aspect of Prairie life as clearly as the Winnipeg General Strike of 1919, a collision of desperation and determination.

Winnipeg's metals and building trades went on strike over union recognition and collective bargaining on May 1. A mass sympathy strike on May 15 kept 22,000 workers out of their workplaces — half of them nonunionized. Police and the waterworks crews kept working, with other essential services permitted to function as needed. Such an event doesn't occur in a vacuum: the employers and the affected levels of government feared the strike was manipulated by communist forces (the Russian Revolution was only a few years old, so the privileged status quo was still pretty touchy). While this strike went on, working Canadians in other cities held "sympathy strikes." In Vancouver,

7

12,000 workers walked off the job. It's easy to romanticize the strike. The fact is, it was tough going for all involved. Families were without income. Owners were without profit. Something had to give, and on June 21 it did.

The sympathetic city police had already been replaced by a special police force created to deal with the strikers. That force couldn't handle the crowd at a June 21 parade, and the Royal North West Mounted Police were sent in. The climate for conflict heated up with the presence of a railcar manned by anti-strikers (of which there were many throughout the dispute). Some of the strikers tipped the railcar over. Police used bats to club down strikers. When one police horse tripped, the crowd attacked the rider, and the police fired into the crowd. The result: two strikers killed and 20 injured. Half a dozen mounted police and special constables were also wounded. This was Bloody Saturday.

 **Moose Jaw's name may have come from a settler who used a moose's jaw to fix a broken cart, or it may have come from *moosegaw*, the Cree word meaning "warm breezes."**

The strikers returned to work on June 25. Hundreds were fired rather than taken back. All had to deal with the impact of having gone six weeks without income. Ottawa's parliamentarians amended the Criminal Code so that several strike leaders could be charged with seditious conspiracy. Two years later, one of them, J. S. Woodsworth, would become the first socialist elected to the House of Commons. This was one of those (then) rare instances of the little guy raising his voice. The fact that other workers in other cities added their voices suggests this was more than just a dispute over work and wages. It was a nationwide expression of working-class discontent, and it paved the way for the modern labour movement in Canada.

"We need money," J. Toothill told the 3,000 people who had gathered in Regina's Market Square on July 1, 1935. This was not exactly news. Everyone needed money back then, and few were as keenly aware of it as the 2,000 men who had hopped eastbound boxcars that June as part of the On to Ottawa Trek. These young men had grown tired of Prime Minister R. B. Bennett's relief camps offering 20 cents a day. After a two-month protest in Vancouver, they took their message to Ottawa, doubling in number along the way. When Bennett directed the Canadian Pacific Railway to ban them as passengers, the march stalled in Regina. For the latter part of June, the men lived peacefully in a stadium at the Exhibition Grounds while their leaders travelled to Ottawa to meet with Bennett. They returned empty-handed, but on July 1 the leaders told the Saskatchewan premier, James Gardiner, they would disband the march and return home. The same day, Bennett directed Regina constables and RCMP officers to arrest trek leader Arthur "Slim" Evans and other speakers.

Seconds after Toothill began his speech, two whistles sounded, and police poured out of three large vans parked at the rear of the crowd. This ill-conceived action initiated the Regina Riot, three hours of fighting between police and civilians that saw 118 men arrested and left more than 100 injured. The two fatalities were Detective Charlie Millar and 52-year-old trekker Nick Schaack, both of whom died from head injuries sustained during the melee.

Many of the people injured that day were Regina citizens. The crowd in Market Square contained only about 300 trekkers: the rest were watching a ball game at Exhibition Stadium. Within days, the trekkers left Regina and returned home — as they had told Gardiner they would, before Bennett brought in the iron fist. Three months later, Bennett was voted out of office. His successor, William Lyon Mackenzie King, shut down the relief camps.

Canadian socialism took root in the farm provinces, perhaps as a substitute for the wheat that was so disastrously absent during the 1930s. The CCF laid out its vision in 1933 in the Regina Manifesto:

The new social order at which we aim is not one in which individuality will be crushed out by a system of regimentation. Nor shall we interfere with cultural rights of racial or religious minorities. What we seek is a proper collective organization of our economic resources such as will make possible a much greater degree of leisure and a much richer individual life for every citizen.

Universal health care is as much a part of being Canadian as trying to understand the off-side rules in hockey. It demonstrates a very Canuck view of society — one based on cooperation and compassion. It's easy to take it for granted, but the idea was so radical when proposed in Saskatchewan in 1962 that the province's doctors went on strike for a month.

The hard years of the 1930s, the scarcity of rural health care and the election of the Co-operative Commonwealth Federation in 1944 all came together to create the impetus toward creating a better health care system. In 1945, the Swift Current Regional Health District was formed as a pilot project to provide prepaid hospital insurance; local taxpayers paid premiums and the municipality in turn paid a fee-for-service to the hospital doctors. In 1947, Tommy Douglas, the CCF premier and health minister, carved the whole province into health regions offering limited medical coverage, paid for through premiums and provincial grants. Ten years later, Ottawa added its two cents worth (well, more than that, although in recent years it's been edging back down toward two cents) and began paying half the costs of running the hospitals in every province.

The CCF was still in power on July 1, 1962, when Saskatchewan launched the first universal medicare plan in North America by expanding medical insurance to include payment for visits to the doctor. This promptly triggered a strike by 90 percent of the province's physicians. The provincial legislators ended the strike on August 2 by agreeing to some minor amendments to mollify the doctors. However, the basic, revolutionary change had been achieved. In 1968, Ottawa introduced medicare nationwide. But in Saskatchewan, more than in any other province, health care transcends social policy. It's part of the culture.

THE EDMONTON FILE

The gateway to the North is also Canada's most northern big city. Indians had lived in the region for thousands of years, but it was the fur-trading rivalry that led to concentrated settlement. The North West Company built a fur-trading post called Fort Augustus (near what's now Fort Saskatchewan) in 1795. The Hudson's Bay Company responded with Fort Edmonton the same year, named after the English birthplace of Sir James Winter Lake, the HBC's deputy governor.

In 1896, Skookum Jim Mason, Dawson Charlie and George Washington Carmack found a yellow rock in the Yukon, and the Klondike Gold Rush was on. Thousands of miners moved through Edmonton on their way to riches, disappointment, and scurvy. Edmonton became a city in 1904, and the next year it was named capital of the infant province of Alberta. When oil was discovered in neighbouring Leduc in 1947, the city developed yet another personality. The hundreds of oil and gas wells surrounding the city continue to provide employment for thousands (and to contribute to Edmonton's reputation as a "blue-collar town"), but today the local economy is powered by other sectors. Through the heady decade of the on-ice dominance of the Oilers in the 1980s and the perennial strong showing by the Eskimos football club, Edmonton has earned a nickname it clearly relishes — the City of Champions. It's also one of the prettier cities you'll see, thanks to the river valley. Speaking to an audience in 1994, Alberta-born folk singer Joni Mitchell commented: "Thank you, Edmonton, for your warmth, your beautiful vista, and your cycling trails."

Some people say Moose Jaw residents are called Moose Javians. That's wishful thinking. The real term is _Moosichappishanissippians_.

A Helping Hand

Maybe because we've always cast ourselves in the role of underdog, and have always had to battle some external nuisance, whether it's cold winds from the north or hot air from Ottawa, Prairie people always find their greatest strength when they come together. Around here, the driver of the minivan with the flat tire doesn't have to flag down help. Chances are that another motorist has already pulled over, jack in hand. For example, based on per capita donations, Saskatchewan's annual Kinsmen Telemiracle is the most successful telethon _in the world_. Yes, there's a definite western individualism, particularly in Alberta, but it's tempered by a cooperative spirit that is decades old.

Cold land; warm hearts. Doubt it? Then check out Statistics Canada's 2000 survey of charitable giving. The Prairies were the most generous region by far. Manitoba led all provinces with an average annual donation of $383 per person. Alberta followed with $369, while Saskatchewan placed a respectable fifth with an average annual gift of $273 per person.

But it's hard to match the generosity of Manitoba's Mennonite communities. According to a 1994 Stats Can survey, the average annual median donation in Morden was $600. Steinbach donors gave $980. Hearts and pocketbooks opened widest in Winkler, where the median charitable donation reached $1,030.

11

When a record-busting snowstorm hit Calgary in mid-March 1998, stories of selflessness emerged that were anything but surprising. Car dealerships lent four-wheel-drive vehicles so volunteers could deliver meals to 600 house-bound seniors. Calgarian Jim Dale drove from snowbank to snowbank, pulling out cars with his half-ton. "I can't do much work today, so I figured I may as well help out," he explained.

White Hats — Black Chapter

While our collective social conscience has led us toward admirable goals, it's also true the Prairies have occasionally been burdened with some backward thinking, and I'm not talking about suspenders.

The Ku Klux Klan moved into Alberta from British Columbia in 1925. The Klan quickly tapped into WASPs' simmering resentment of European immigrants and French-Canadian Catholicism and drove its membership up to around 5,000. The first known cross-burning occurred on November 1, 1929, in Drumheller. The Klan was soon backing the Progressive Conservative Party and even burned a cross to celebrate the victory of Tory Ambrose Bury as MP for East Edmonton in 1930. By the middle of that lean, dry decade, people had bigger problems than the Klan could even pretend to solve. Public scandal among the hate group's leadership contributed to a widespread drop in its influence and membership.

Premier Pat Binns of Prince Edward Island was born in Weyburn, Saskatchewan, and raised in Radville.

However, Saskatchewan proved even more fertile ground for the Klan's message. On June 7, 1927, more than 5,000 people gathered in Moose Jaw to attend the Klan's first public rally in the province. The exact membership in Saskatchewan has never been pinned down, but it numbered at least 10,000 and perhaps as many as 50,000. Klan leaders spoke on a variety of topical issues, but anti-Catholic and anti-immigrant intolerance wasn't exactly buried. Nor was it masked in euphemism. Speaking to a crowd in Moose Jaw, organizer J. H. Hawkins referred to the "scum that refuse to assimilate." Some Protestant clergymen spoke proudly of their Klan affiliation. Klan members worked behind the scenes at Tory party conventions in the late 1920s and were a significant factor in the unprecedented (for Saskatchewan) election of a Tory government in 1929. The organization's demise was as rapid as its ascent. The Klan's venomous tirades prompted equally passionate reactions, and opposition to the Klan intensified. Leader J. J. Maloney was decorated with rotten eggs during a 1928 address in Meota. Infighting and scandal among the Klan leadership, coupled with the public's growing disinterest in the targets that the Klan claimed were so threatening, hastened the end. Membership waned, and the Klan's annual provincial meeting in January 1930 proved to be its last in that province. Thankfully.

THE ONLY SHIP ON THE PRAIRIES — FRIENDSHIP

This oft-repeated story of the Manitoba "seeding bee" epitomizes the neighbourly camaraderie that we like to think is a little more common around here than in most places.

According to lore, a Ukrainian farmer ruptured his appendix at the worst possible time: the start of seeding. The next day, every farmer in the district put aside the demands of his own land and converged on the ill man's farm. The men plowed, harrowed, and seeded their neighbour's fields. At noon they sat down to a feast prepared by the women of the area. The day of labour turned into a social event, one that sowed more than wheat.

Calgary cattleman-meat packer Pat Burns (1856–1937) once sent two workmen to Midnapore to apply a fresh coat of paint to the weathered Catholic church there. When Burns journeyed to the small town to check on their progress, he was delighted with the result. However, he noticed that the nearby Protestant church, already showing its age, only looked that much shabbier in comparison. Burns discreetly directed the workmen to cross the street and paint it, and to do just as good a job.

THE CALGARY FILE

Calgary's status as a booming city of clean streets and gleaming glass buildings was recognized when producers of the 1978 film *Superman* chose the rapidly growing municipality to play the role of Metropolis, the ultramodern home of Clark Kent and his alter ego.

The growth spurt of the 1960s and 1970s has been emulated in the 1990s. In 1997 alone, 40,000 people moved there to bask in the warm glow of the sunny economy. As its population edges toward one million, Calgary is wearing its jewellery again: new cars drive past new buildings and return to new homes. This boom, coupled with the

13

lingering satisfaction of hosting the 1988 Winter Olympics and the annual chest-puffing celebration that is the Calgary Stampede, have cultivated a sense of civic pride unrivalled in the country.

Built at the convergence of the Bow and Elbow Rivers as a Mountie settlement in 1876, Fort Calgary is Gaelic for "bay farm." The city is at the epicentre of Alberta's ranchland, giving it the nickname Cowtown. Like Edmonton, it has benefited greatly from the discovery of large oil fields in 1947. The entrepreneurship even extends into romance: Calgary has a vibrant dating scene (my single friends tell me).

Only on the Prairies?

And you thought Via Rail was underutilized ... The only UFO landing pad in the world sits at St. Paul, Alberta. It was built in 1967 as a centennial project. According to Jules J. Van Brabant, the town's mayor at the time, the idea arose during beer-drinking. "I thought it was a little far-fetched, but everyone was a little far-fetched that night," he remembers. What Van Brabant and the others came up with was a 12-metre-wide wooden circular platform, raised above ground level and adorned with provincial and territorial flags. So far the only visitors have been tourists; in 1998 the town hosted its first UFO convention. Still, the people of St. Paul remain at the ready. We Prairie folks figure crop circles are a sign that (1) there are other intelligent beings in the universe and (2) they're farmers.

St. Paul didn't come up with the oddest centennial celebration. That honour probably goes to Wabowden, Manitoba. The town's project was sensible enough: the switch to indoor plumbing. However, the residents celebrated the event by burning their suddenly outdated outhouses.

Sometimes we're not who we appear. The most famous example was surely Grey Owl, the internationally known author and wildlife conservationist who lived in the woods of Manitoba and Saskatchewan during much of the first half of the century. During the 1930s, he was a wildly celebrated character who toured the world in long braids and buckskin as he preached his message to save the wilderness and its inhabitants, notably the beaver. His death on April 19, 1938, was reported around the world. Within days, an odd story emerged on the other side of the Atlantic. A British woman named Ada Belaney told British journalists that Grey Owl had been her nephew.

14

"Archie was an ordinary English boy with a vivid imagination and passionate fondness for animals," she said. Her allegations gained weight when a woman who claimed to be Archibald Belaney's first wife told the press that the fourth toe on his right foot had been amputated following a war wound. The funeral home in Prince Albert checked the corpse and reported that the digit in question was indeed absent. Despite the many people who came forward to say they had personally known Grey Owl as a Native, or a "half-breed," he was, in fact, Archibald Belaney, born in Hastings, England, in 1888. The son of an American woman and a British doctor moved to Canada when he was 17, returned to England for a brief, unsuccessful marriage, and journeyed back to Canada to reinvent himself.

The unveiling of his true heritage explains why, when Grey Owl toured England, he frequently asked if there were any Belaneys in the audience. And why this supposedly full-blooded Ojibway sometimes spoke with an English accent.

Notions Near and Dear

One issue above all else is capable of tying Saskatchewan into a knot. It's not the death of the Crow rate or the Roughriders' perennial quarterback controversy. It's time.

Specifically daylight savings time. Saskatchewan is the one province that doesn't tamper with the clock. For six months of the year, it shares Alberta's schedule. During the winter months, it ticks and tocks in time with Manitoba.

Many right-thinking folks, and I number myself among them, wonder what would be so bad about an extra hour of daylight in summer, so we can go for walks or play tennis well into the evening? Conversely what's so great about sunlight at 5 a.m.?

Manitoba was the first province to give women the vote, in January 1916. Within three months, Saskatchewan and Alberta followed suit.

Such comments always prompt a chorus of disapproval from people, many of them seniors and farmers, who staunchly want to preserve the chronological status quo. Their most common charge is that changing the clocks would confuse the cows, which are milked on a fairly rigid schedule. They also point out that Saskatchewan is already on daylight savings time, all the time, and that proponents of a change are actually calling for *double daylight savings time*.

Fine, but I come back to my question, what would be so bad about an extra hour of sunlight during summer?

 **In 1922 Regina city council passed bylaw 1097, establishing an annual licensing fee of $300 for "every person practising the art or profession of a Phrenologist."**

Albertans take understandable comfort — and even pride — in the fact that they alone have no sales tax. And don't even think of suggesting there should be one.

The reason is simply that Alberta doesn't need it. The earnings on the oil and gas revenues that have filled the Alberta Heritage Savings Trust Fund since 1976 provide the provincial government with as much revenue as a modest sales tax.

Next-Year Country

I'm not sure who first came up with the phrase, but it's not hard to imagine what motivated him or her. Maybe next year drought won't dry out the land. Maybe next year it won't freeze early. Maybe next year there won't be grasshoppers, or weeds, or gophers, or hail. Maybe next year the wind won't damage the crop. And if it does? Well, what else are you going to do? Besides, there's always the year after that.

THE REGINA FILE

The word *regina* is Latin for "queen." The city was named in 1882 for Queen Victoria. The original First Nations name, Wascana, means "pile of bones," so named for the skeletal bison remains once placed there in honour of the creature so central to Great Plains Indian life.

Regina's great curse has been that its location was determined through the machinations of CPR bigwig and future lieutenant governor Edgar Dewdney. To ensure the new town was built on land belonging to him and his pals (thereby jacking up its value), he worked to have the rail line laid where it is rather than along the

more logical and lovely setting of the Qu'Appelle Valley, 40 kilometres to the north. As such, Regina is the only major Canadian city not
built on a significant waterway. (The pretty but unswimmable Wascana
Lake was created by pinching Wascana Creek, the modest stream that
winds through the surrounding fields.)

Regina became the capital of the enormous North-West
Territories in 1883. In 1905 it became the capital of the new province
of Saskatchewan. With no river valley or nearby mountains, Regina
is a city of hidden pleasures as subtle and sweet as a cool breeze. The
one not-so-hidden characteristic is the roar of 25,000 voices cheering
on the Saskatchewan Roughriders at Taylor Field.

Odd Laws for Odd Times

Saskatoon's 1909 bylaw relating to public morals was a sweeping piece of
local legislation intended to curb all manner of human misadventure, whether
it be vagrancy, gambling, indecency, or drunkenness. Or swimming. Bylaw
260 prohibited anyone from bathing in the Saskatchewan River "unless wearing a proper bathing dress, covering the body from the neck to the knees."
And not after 11 p.m.!

Saskatchewan does not allow the consumption of alcohol in strip bars, effectively keeping them out of business. The legislation was carried to its
extreme when a liquor inspector ruled in the early 1990s that an aerobic dance
display inside a music festival's beer tent broke the law because the participants
wore spandex. To the rest of Canada, Saskatchewan looked a bit, um, uptight.

Flash forward to 1998, when a Regina judge ruled that two women were
innocent of indecent exposure when they suntanned topless. That's a long
journey in a few scant years. I think stripping remains forbidden largely
because no legislative backbencher wants to be the one who stands up and
introduces a bill to legalize it. ("Mr. Speaker. Whereas every other province
allows exotic dancing in licensed establishments, and Whereas my cousin
Rudy has a bachelor party coming up ...")

Our politicians constantly balance moral modernization with the rural
values that still exist in communities large and small. Curiously Saskatchewan's
NDP government has doggedly promoted the spread of video lottery terminals
and the construction of several large casinos during the 1990s. That's the same
Department of Justice that has prosecuted bar owners who defied the anti-
stripping legislation. I guess we can lose our shirts; we just can't take them off.

The Flatlander's Calendar

We don't have to scour the wilds for housing materials or fetch water from a well anymore, but Prairie folk still face more hardships than any other group in Canada, with the possible exception of Blue Jays fans. Okay, so maybe people won't call us pioneers, but they should at least appreciate what we have to put up with. Here, then, is a Prairie calendar.

- October to March: winter, sometimes referred to as three of the four seasons. The silver lining is that January is so cold the entire region resembles a giant cryogenics lab, and for those horrible 31 days metabolism slows and people don't age.
- April: the thaw. Move everything valuable out of the basement. The car may need a wash.
- May: tiny worms hang from silver strands and ruin the nice walk in the park that we've dreamed about for the past six months.
- June to August: so many mosquitoes, so little ointment.
- September: check the block heater. Buy a new winter coat. Stack the firewood. Store nuts.

Laughing All the Way to the Food Bank

A Department of Agriculture employee surveying Saskatoon in the 1930s reported that windstorms had blown away everything except "the mortgages and the farmers' sense of humour." One farmer who finally decided to pull up stakes in 1938 and look elsewhere for better prospects painted his hard-luck tale on the side of a wagon: "1930 — Frozen out ... 1932 — Hailed out ... 1936 — Rusted out ... 1937 — Dried out ... 1938 — Moving the hell out."

Our parched soil created an equally dry sense of humour. It may have started as a coping mechanism, but it has stayed with us, long after times finally took a turn for the better.

> "I have a kind of a dry, crop-failure sense of humour."
> — *Connie Kaldor, Saskatchewan-born singer-songwriter*

The wildness of our history, from voyageurs to cowboys, has bred a harmless nonconformity that probably wouldn't be tolerated in more stiff-necked eastern cities. A case in point was lawyer Frank Cornish, Winnipeg's first mayor. According to one story, Cornish was sitting as police magistrate one morning when he called his own name. He laid a charge against himself for driving a carriage while drunk. Cornish stood up, left his seat, and pleaded guilty, his head bowed down in remorse. He fined himself $5. Then, noting this was his first offence, he cancelled the fine.

Alberta's provincial bird is the great horned owl, the official flower is the wild rose, and the official mammal is the bighorn sheep.

THE SASKATOON FILE

Called the Bridge City because of the seven varied and scenic structures that span the South Saskatchewan River, Saskatoon is a charming small city with natural beauty and the hip sensibility that comes from hosting a large university.

Saskatoon's origin is unique. In 1882 a congregation of more than 100 Methodists led by John Lake was granted 81,000 hectares to build a community true to their beliefs. This meant that, among other things, the new municipality would practise temperance. Originally named Minnetonka, after a local lake, the city was redubbed for the sweet berry that grew in abundance. The eventual wave of immigrants diluted the Methodists' influence, and the temperance colony evolved into a modern city.

The rivalry between Saskatchewan's two largest cities is rooted in the fact that one was named the capital and the other was given the University of Saskatchewan. If Regina is a "sports town," then Saskatoon is an artsier burg, as proven by its many music and theatre festivals.

Intercity rivalry exists around the world, and we're no exception. When Regina was chosen as the capital of the North-West Territories, the editor of the *Manitoba Free Press* cited the lack of trees and natural water and concluded that "it would scarcely make a respectable farm ... The place has not a single natural advantage to commend it."

The editor of the *Brandon Sun* had obviously grown tired of his community's secondary status when he wrote about the gumbo that jeopardized Winnipeg's expanding network of streets: "The people of Winnipeg are at a loss to know what to do with Main Street. They have abandoned the notion

of gravelling it, and block paving will cost more than they can stand ...
The best thing they can do is move out of the place."

Prairie fashion is unique, probably because no one else wants it. It's like the people who wear it. Simple and practical. In many towns, the closest thing to a boutique is the rack of new flannels at the Saan store. The biggest designer name around here? John Deere, worn high on the head, and don't bend the brim. While European and New York designers switch stylistic allegiances annually, we remain pretty faithful to plaid. But like those fancy designers, we believe in layers. In winter anyway.

The values of the men and women who ride horses for a living, for sport, and for peace of mind are succinctly captured in the Cowboy's Prayer. It can be found on grave markers throughout western cemeteries.

> Heavenly Father, we pause, mindful
> of the many blessings you have bestowed upon us.
> We ask that you be with us at this rodeo,
> and we pray that you will guide us in the arena of life.
> Help us Lord to live our lives in such a manner
> that when we make the last inevitable ride
> to the country up there, where the grass grows
> lush green and stirrup-high,
> and the water runs cool, clear, and deep,
> that you, as our last judge, will tell us
> that our entry fees are paid.

Chapter 2

Where We Came From

STAN CUTHAND: TELLING STORIES

Poundmaker was a womanizer. A ladies' man. This is not the sort of tidbit that turns up in history books. But it was a fact, asserts Stan Cuthand. He learned about Poundmaker, a pivotal figure in the Northwest Rebellion, from his father, who learned it from his father, who saw it firsthand. Oral tradition is storytelling based on experience. As a result, it is less the study of great men — the very nature of Euro-Canadian history — than a remembrance of the everyday experiences of the people. Assemble enough of these stories and you have a firsthand account of all the major events of the Prairies in the 19th and 20th centuries.

Although oral tradition is not about to transform history classes in the public school system, Reverend Cuthand is hopeful that the First Nations perspective will at least become better understood among Native and non-Native students alike now that it is being taught in high schools. For example, Canadian history portrays the arrival of the Mounted Police as a necessary step to save Prairie First Nations from the cruelty and avarice of American whisky traders. "That's one theory," says Cuthand. "They didn't. They came to protect the settlers." From the Natives, who inspired fear because of the violence that had occurred south of the border during the "Indian Wars" with the U.S. cavalry. Another view is that Ottawa wanted to affirm the border with an armed presence across the west to prevent incursions by expansionist Americans.

"Oral tradition comes from firsthand experience," Cuthand says. He taught Indian Studies at the Saskatoon campus of the Saskatchewan Indian Federated College (SIFC) until his retirement in 1999. ("You can't call it history, because the historians will be angry," he says, smiling.) Mainstream historians like to dismiss anything that's not recorded on paper. Oral tradition is seen as vulnerable to exaggeration, inaccuracy, and prejudice, as if academic views of World War II and the Cold War were not vulnerable to subjective theories and political biases. "They always thought oral tradition wasn't reliable, but anthropologists studied it and found 80 percent of it is accurate," Cuthand says.

Two things crippled First Nations life across the Prairies. The first thing was the disappearance of the buffalo. The twin forces of hunting and buffalo migration that had balanced each other for centuries were upset by white settlement. Bison were killed with excessive zeal and efficiency, often for no more than sport, and carcasses rotted on the ground. The second thing, more premeditated, was the use of treaties to secure unopposed management of the landscape and the subsequent suppression of Indian culture. Overt cultural expressions such as the Sun Dance were banned. Many Native children were removed from their families and placed in religious boarding schools.

But today, all around, there are encouraging signs. Some suggest that First Nations people have learned a thing or two from the people who displaced them, including the need to assert their economic power in order to strengthen their culture. "We're buying land. That's a great step," Cuthand says. In some cases, the new landlords rent out the land to the former owners, who get to keep farming it. There is talk of local self-government on urban reserves for economic development and of an alternative justice system for Natives. In fact, sentencing circles have already appeared in an effort to identify a more productive punishment than incarceration. And, of course, SIFC attracts students from across the country, educating them with the written and the spoken word.

22

The history of white and First Nations relations is marked with misunderstanding and conflict, and that won't change overnight, but Cuthand is heartened by the sight of Native people opening once-closed doors of influence, all the while retaining their own ways. "Catching up to a culture that's 1,000 years old, we're doing really well."

Canada's first Mormon temple was built in 1923 in Cardston, Alberta.

Reverend Cuthand told his children the stories that he had learned as a boy. His son Doug produced a TV miniseries about Big Bear. The $8.5 million production was shot in Saskatchewan in the spring of 1998. The reverend's son is using 20th-century communications technology to tell the story he learned at his father's knee.

"If you have a society where they don't have written words, and they learn by oral tradition, you have a long memory, because the stories are told and retold," Stan says. "The children have a good memory. They're good listeners."

Some Early Residents

The Prairies have supported animal life for more than 200 million years. The Albertosaurus dates back to the Mesozoic age, which lasted from 225 million B.C. to 65 million B.C. Of course, any dinosaur named after Alberta would have been a carnivore. It roamed the marshes of the province's southeastern region, looking for prey. It's tempting to draw a parallel between Alberta's shoot-from-the-hip politicians and the 7.5-metre-tall beast with a thick neck and a large but lightly constructed skull. But that would be insensitive.

The province's capital is appropriately represented by a mild-mannered, slumbering reptile. The Edmontonosaurus was nine metres long, with a duck-like bill and a horselike head.

About 50 kilometres northeast of Brooks, a motorist can drive through arable fields and over the crest of a typically modest Alberta hill to come face to face with a view suggesting that he or she has just passed through a time-space portal.

Dinosaur Provincial Park is a geological anomaly. In the middle of the prairie, this vast stretch of otherworldly rock walls and sandstone valleys resembles a Not-Quite-as-Grand Canyon. In fact, it's a 76-million-year-old cemetery. Since excavation began in the 1880s, more than 300 complete skeletons have been found here. No other area in the world has produced such a variety of fossils in such a small area. For millions of years, rivers carried sediment into the prehistoric sea that once covered the Great Plains. The debris carried along in those rivers was deposited here and eventually fossilized. Some of the park's 60,000 annual visitors stumble across these intriguing stone snapshots. In 1995 fossil finders uncovered a pristine skeleton of the ornithomimid, a prehistoric ostrich.

Water from a retreating glacier carved the badlands in Alberta more than 10,000 years ago.

Alberta has a second famous dinosaur site. About 150 kilometres northeast of Calgary lies Drumheller, a community set amid a positively Martian landscape. A few millenniums of erosion have shaped a topography marked by strange rock formations. The sharp-eyed can find dinosaur fossils from the Cretaceous age. The Royal Tyrrell Museum of Paleontology explains the whole story, and it's a lot more entertaining than the *Jurassic Park* sequels.

Biting Off as Much as It Could Chew

Scientists were delighted in 1998 by the discovery of a 60-centimetre piece of fossilized dung in southwest Saskatchewan. I guess they don't get out much. Because of its impressive size, researchers deduced that the Jurassic poop came from a Tyrannosaurus Rex or some other 20-metre-tall carnivore. The finding has already provided them with new knowledge about the dinosaur's dining habits. Scientists had believed that the T-Rex tore its prey apart and then swallowed large pieces, but small bone fragments in the feces suggest that the beast chewed and crushed the food and that its stomach never completely digested the contents.

Also, they think that T-Rex could have used more fibre in its diet.

The First People

They were immigrants too. The most popular theory suggests that First Nations peoples came here from Asia 12,000 years ago. They crossed via the land link that existed where the Bering Strait now lies, before the end of the last ice age

24

melted the glaciers and buried the bridge under water. Archeologists have found plenty of Homo sapien skeletons in North America, but they have never found the remains of an older species of humans. The conclusion is that the first people came here from elsewhere.

First Nations initially tracked bison on foot, literally sneaking up on them until they were close enough to use an arrow or spear. When the horse arrived in 1750, they climbed on top and gained the advantage of speed. One of the most effective and ingenious hunting methods was the bison jump. Sped on by warriors disguised as wolves, the frightened animals were herded for many kilometres toward a sharp cliff over which they fell to their deaths. It sounds messy and cruel, but it was surprisingly effective. Peter Fidler, one of the first white settlers to spend any time with the First Nations people, watched a small bison jump and reported that 29 were killed on the spot. Only three survived, but they had broken legs and were quickly overtaken and killed.

The best-known of these jumps is Head-Smashed-In Buffalo Jump, a UNESCO World Heritage Site that, besides being smartly presented, benefits from a scenic location west of Fort Macleod, in the foothills of southwestern Alberta. One might assume that the jump's name stems from the animals' fate. Nope. About 150 years ago, a curious young brave positioned himself at the base of the jump, his back pressed against the cliff wall so that he could watch the kill. At first, the ledge overhead sheltered him from the avalanche of mammoth bodies. As the carcasses piled up, however, the brave became trapped and was quickly buried under them. When the hunters discovered his body, they saw that his head had been smashed in.

The Treaties

As Prime Minister John A. Macdonald worked to put the new nation in order, he concerned himself with settling and exploiting the newly purchased Rupert's Land, bringing British Columbia into the fledgling nation and building the railway that would unite the country. The needs of the First Nations people weren't as high a priority. In fact, the most momentous political influence ever demonstrated by Native people might have been on June 23, 1990, when MLA Elijah Harper rose in the Manitoba legislature and refused to provide the unanimous support required to pass the Meech Lake Accord.

Between 1871 and 1877, Ottawa pushed for and obtained the signing of the first seven numbered treaties. These agreements were intended to confine

60,000 Plains Indians to reserves without waging costly and bloody wars like those that had occurred throughout the southwestern United States. In all, there would be 11 numbered treaties governing the first inhabitants of the Plains. To understand how they generally worked, consider the exchange rate laid out in Treaty 7. The Blackfoot accepted the reserves, livestock, farm equipment, ammunition, and payments in exchange for 128,000 square kilometres of southern Alberta.

Plains Cree is the single biggest Aboriginal group in each of the three Prairie provinces. Alberta is also home to the Blackfoot, who are actually three nations (the Siksikah, the Blood, and the Peigan), Dakota, South Slave, Chipewyan, Ojibway (also known as Saulteaux), and Inuktitut. Ojibway, Dakota, Chipewyan, and Inuktitut are the other major groups in both Saskatchewan and Manitoba, although smaller nations exist in each of the three provinces.

Les Voyageurs

I have camped often enough to know that the life of the voyageur was not nearly as romantic as it is often depicted. Sure, there were plenty of peaceful canoe rides into the fur-bearing lands of the Plains Indians. And the guys probably looked fashionably rugged in their buckskins. But they also lived a gruelling and dangerous existence that often left them cold, sick, and less well fed than the mosquitoes that feasted on them. These hardy souls were the middlemen between the First Nations hunters and the eastern fur merchants, and they were the first whites to conduct business on the Prairies. Each February, their contribution is celebrated at the Festival du Voyageur in the French community of St. Boniface in eastern Winnipeg. In recognition of *les voyageurs'* lifestyle, the festival includes a beard-growing contest.

The story of Canada cannot be told without the use of two acronyms, one well known and the other consigned to the history books. The first is HBC. The Hudson's Bay Company was chartered in London in 1670: today Canadians know it simply as The Bay. Created precisely to exploit the resource goodies in North America, the company enjoyed vast powers granted to it by King Charles II, including exclusive trading rights. The company's interest in Rupert's Land was almost solely as a source of furs for European consumers. The HBC's dealings were repeatedly disrupted by French fur traders, a competition that even instigated naval and land battles in the early 18th century.

The second acronym is NWC: the North West Company. From 1780 to 1821, the NWC was the HBC's biggest rival. The fur-trade exporter was run by Montreal-based Scots. Aggressive exploration into the continent's heartland gave the firm control over two-thirds of Canada's fur trade by 1795. However, the HBC was able to exert pressure by choking off the Nor'Westers' supply lines.

The two firms merged under the HBC's name in 1821, bringing an end to the competition that had spurred western exploration. The HBC oversaw its massive western operations from a head office in Fort Garry. The scope of the HBC's royal charter made it the de facto government across Rupert's Land. Just as the fur trade was cooling off, the HBC sold its land to the new nation of Canada but retained five percent of the arable land being opened for settlement as well as its many trading posts. The company was thereby able to become a major land developer on the rapidly growing Prairies. The settlers who moved onto the land needed supplies, and the HBC set up stores to sell them. The Prairies became the HBC's market rather than its supplier. One hundred years later, Prairie shoppers wander through the aisles of HBC stores with scarcely any knowledge of the company's role in our history.

In August 1961, Lake Athabasca surrendered the biggest lake trout ever caught — 46 kilograms of fish!

The Red River Colony was really ground zero for European settlement of the Prairies. Fur traders had ventured much farther west during the 18th century, but the Red River settlement was the first attempt at any kind of community. The fifth Earl of Selkirk, Thomas Douglas, was granted 300,000 square kilometres of land from the Hudson's Bay Company in 1811. He envisioned a settlement in an area to be called Assiniboia, enveloping the region where the Red and Assiniboine Rivers forked. The Red River settlement was born in August 1812, when the first settlers arrived. Imagine how it must have felt to leave the comforts of what was then considered the height of civilization in order to pitch tents in the middle of a field. Imagine how their doubts must have been compounded during that first winter!

Canada's Distinct People: The Métis

It's been suggested that the Métis appeared nine months after the first time a European explorer met a North American Native woman. The Métis of the Prairies were born of the blending of two cultures, but the mixed-blood background eventually evolved into a unique sociocultural group, one whose members spoke French, English, or a dialect called Mischif. They built their first communities in the Assiniboia region of southern Manitoba, although many picked up and headed for north-central Saskatchewan in the late 19th century.

Today nearly two-thirds of Canada's 292,300 Métis live in the Prairie provinces. Nearly 41 percent of Métis adults participate in traditional practices such as hunting, trapping, fiddle-playing, and storytelling. In fact, younger Métis are even more involved in such activities. Métis culture is very much alive.

Louis Riel wasn't the first leader of the Métis. Cuthbert Grant's mother was only partly Cree, with very little French background, and his father was a Scot, yet Grant was regarded as the first head of the Red River Métis. A senior NWC executive took the young Métis to Montreal to receive a private education. Grant continued his studies in Scotland and eventually returned to the west to work as a clerk for the fur-trading company. He was politicized by a proclamation from Robert Semple, the governor of the pro-HBC Red River Colony, that prohibited the export of pemmican, the year-round staple of NWC traders. Grant organized Métis to oppose the ruling. Some simply took pemmican by force. Tensions turned to hostilities, culminating in the Battle of Seven Oaks, also known as the Seven Oaks Massacre, depending on which side of the bullet you stood. Semple and a party of his settlers encountered Métis, led by Grant, who were transporting pemmican to an NWC post on June 19, 1816. Amid much confusion, someone fired a shot, and both sides were quickly drawn into battle. In the end, Semple and 20 of his men were dead. There was only one Métis casualty, and before long there was at least one folk song celebrating the Métis victory. Regardless of which side won, this confrontation was surely the nadir of the competition between the two fur-trading giants.

Loyalty to his people and to the North West Company — and his involvement at Seven Oaks — made Grant the settlers' foe for years. However, after the HBC and the NWC merged in 1821, he swore off violent actions and would later befriend the colony's new governor, George Simpson.

Grant settled on a patch of land along the Assiniboine, 24 kilometres west of the Forks, and soon attracted other Métis, who moved there and set up an agricultural community known as Grantown. The once-feared Métis were eventually perceived as a stabilizing influence who would protect themselves

— and the white Red River settlers — from the threat posed by American Sioux. Grant built a flour mill and worked as a doctor in the region, but he is best known for the position that he assumed in 1828: "Warden of the Plains." It was his duty to prevent illegal fur trading. Despite the buffalo hunter's reputation as a skilled horseman, Grant died after falling from his horse in 1854.

Palliser's Triangle

This phrase turns up in many books about the history of the Plains. It refers to the triangular stretch of prairie land between what is now Brandon, Calgary, and Edmonton that Captain John Palliser dismissed as unsuitable for development. He checked it out during a British expedition to explore North America over a three-year period starting in 1857. As it turns out, Palliser was wrong, and 50 years later his triangle was covered with farmland.

The RCMP's famous musical ride was first performed in the winter of 1887 at the NWMP's riding school in Regina.

Canadian history has its own version of the Louisiana Purchase, only bigger. In 1869, two years after the British North America Act created the Dominion of Canada, the Hudson's Bay Company sold Rupert's Land to the new nation. The cost was £300,000. Today real estate agents occasionally torture themselves by calculating the unclaimed sales commission on that deal.

Three hundred kilometres northeast of Prince Albert lies Cumberland House, the first inland settlement in Rupert's Land. HBC explorer Samuel Hearne established it in 1774 and named it for Prince Rupert, the founder of the trading company and the Duke of Cumberland.

NOT EVEN TIME TO GET THE OFFICIAL MAP PRINTED
For a brief time, a large portion of the Prairies left the British Empire and formed its own country. Well, maybe it was just one guy, and everyone else simply played along for a while. In 1867 shopkeeper Thomas Spence created the Republic of Manitobah and named his home of Portage la Prairie as the capital. The republic stretched west to the Rockies, east to Fort Garry, north to the Arctic Circle, and, because even Spence recognized his limitations, south to

the U.S. border. Manitobah's monetary needs were few, and Spence planned to meet them by collecting duty on incoming goods.

When "President" Spence tried to prosecute a businessman who refused to pay taxes and openly criticized the republic, reality intruded upon his dreamworld. When Spence installed himself as judge at the man's makeshift trial, the accused's angry neighbours forcibly pulled their friend from the dock. A melee ensued, and Spence was run out of town, ending the republic before it was a year old, and thereby leaving all three Prairie provinces free to join Canada when their times came.

The Red Serge

As Stan Cuthand suggests, there are different opinions about why John A. Macdonald really created the North West Mounted Police. What can't be disputed is that some form of authority was needed across the region. Macdonald based the new force on the Royal Irish Constabulatory, the British police force expected to maintain peace and order in Ireland. The stated mission of the Mounties was to stop the whisky trade, reflected at its worst in the ruinous practices at Fort Whoop-Up (near Lethbridge), where primarily American traders took furs from the Blackfoot in exchange for the lowest-grade booze imaginable. Beyond that, they were expected to establish friendly relations with the Natives and maintain the law.

Canada's only *mori* — an Icelandic ghost — is a shy boy spirit in Manitoba.

To appreciate how unruly, amoral, and just plain violent were the traders who worked at Fort Whoop-Up, consider this act recorded in a letter from one employee of the fort to a friend in Montana: he wrote that he had fatally shot his partner for "putting on airs." Then he mentioned that the potatoes were coming along fine.

Cypress Hills Massacre

The same wooded hills that break up the flat lines of southwestern Saskatchewan were the site of a sorrowful but significant event. In 1873 a gang of white wolf hunters, reportedly Americans, got into a liquor-fuelled fight with some Assiniboine. The hunters, who believed that the Natives were responsible for

30

the theft of some horses, killed 20 of the Assiniboine. Only one of the wolf hunters was killed. It was this event that Macdonald used to illustrate the need for a national police force to provide security in the expanding west. The new force built Fort Walsh near the site of the massacre.

Three hundred eastern Canadian men were hired in the first recruitment drive for the North West Mounted Police. The biggest draw was the promise of adventure. It couldn't have been the pay, which was literally "another day, another dollar." A subconstable made even less — 75 cents. But there was food, a bed, and that spiffy red-and-blue uniform. More persuasive was Ottawa's promise of 64 hectares of land after three years of service.

And what was Ottawa looking for? According to the first recruitment ads, the men had to be

- aged 18 to 40
- at least 183 centimetres (six feet) tall
- good horsemen
- of fine character
- active and healthy
- able to read and write English or French.

Arthur H. Griesbad was the first man to sign up for the new police force. The third was Samuel B. Steele. If one Mountie ever looked the part, it was Steele — big, barrel-chested, and mustachioed. The Ontario-born Steele courted a life of adventure like a character from Kipling. He joined the new police force for the Great March West and was named sergeant major in 1873. He was handed his first command at Fort Qu'Appelle the following year. For nearly two decades, Steele policed the Prairies. He became superintendent in 1885 but eschewed any sort of administrative semiretirement, instead becoming the voice of the law and the Canadian government during the untamed era of the Klondike Gold Rush. Steele commanded riflemen in the Boer War and trained Canadian soldiers in England during World War I before retiring in 1918. It clearly wasn't the life for this man of action. He died the following year.

The Thin Red Line

The Great March West was the new police force's baptism by fire. Or, more accurately, its baptism by cold, sickness, and mosquitoes. (Funny how things don't change.) A force of 300 left Fort Garry, Manitoba, on July 8, 1874, and marched west toward southern Alberta. Their final destination turned out to be a fort on an island in the Old Man River. They named it Fort Macleod, in honour of Colonel J. F. Macleod, their commanding officer.

According to John Kittson, the doctor assigned to accompany those first recruits on their foray into the unknown, a litany of illnesses regularly affected the men. In these days before aerosol, the good doctor had the men wear oil of juniper to discourage mosquitoes. For those who were bitten, he recommended liquid ammonia diluted in 10 parts water. In his record of all the afflictions that appeared among the troops during 1875, syphilis ranked fourth, with 14 cases. There were nine cases of gonorrhea, and Kittson wrote that some cases were likely not reported. By 1875 there were 269 men and 26 officers stationed at a series of posts across the Prairies, 140 of them at Fort Macleod.

THE MOUNTIES GOT THEIR FIRST MAN.
THEY JUST COULDN'T KEEP HIM.
The first person arrested by the national force was William Bond, a whisky trader pinched at Pine Coulee, Alberta, in 1873. He escaped to the United States — for good.

The case of the first murdered Mountie has never been solved. Constable Marmaduke Graburn was shot in the back while checking horses in Cypress Hills on November 17, 1879. A Blood named Star Child was acquitted of the murder in 1881.

Regina's history is inextricably linked with the Mounties. In 1920, the year that the force was renamed the Royal Canadian Mounted Police to reflect its role as a truly national police force, the headquarters was moved from Regina to Ottawa. However, the training facility and the museum remain in Regina, and they are still the Queen City's most popular tourist attractions. In fact, when the 1997 Miss Korea was granted a free trip to any destination in the world, she chose Regina because of the RCMP.

Prophet of the New World
It's good that Canadian history is nowhere near as violent as that of the United States, right? Americans were born of a revolution; Canadians have negotiated around tables. They settled the west with sheriffs who faced off against outlaws

in street-level gunfights; we sent in a paramilitary force that spoke first, shot second. They had a civil war; we … well, we sort of had one too. And the individual most often associated with it, Louis Riel, is probably the most fascinating person in Prairie history. For a time, he was probably the most hated man in the country, embodying everything that mainstream Canada was not: (partly) Aboriginal, French-speaking, and Catholic. And yet, 100 years later, he is widely regarded as a Father of Confederation. Certainly Manitoba's creation in 1870 was linked directly to his actions.

Riel was born in St. Boniface in 1844 to a deeply religious Métis family. He was educated in law in Montreal and returned to the Red River area just as Ottawa was preparing to buy Rupert's Land from the Hudson's Bay Company. That change brought surveyors who appeared ready to simply ignore Métis riverfront lots. Only in his mid-20s, Riel set up a provisional government, sparking the Red River Rebellion of 1869-70. The Métis stopped the surveying and seized Fort Garry. Anti-Métis sentiment ranged from understandable concern to blatant racism, the latter embodied by men such as surveyor Thomas Scott, an ill-mannered Ontario Orangeman. He was arrested, released, and arrested again by the Métis for plotting to overthrow the provisional government. The Métis court-martialled and executed Scott, a tragic lapse in judgement by Riel and his supporters. That said, it was largely due to the uprising that Métis language, land ownership, and educational rights were entrenched in the legislation that created the Province of Manitoba in 1870.

Riel fled, living as an exile even after the Métis and Catholic populace elected him to Parliament in 1873 and 1874. The ongoing calls for his arrest for Scott's execution prevented him from ever taking his seat in the House of Commons. Apparently suffering a nervous breakdown, Riel spent some years in a Prairie mental hospital before moving to Montana.

In 1884 Métis hunter Gabriel Dumont left northern Saskatchewan with a delegation to visit Riel in Montana. He asked him to return to Canada to act as the Métis's spokesman regarding several outstanding issues tied to the use of their land and thus their survival. Ignored, Riel once again proclaimed a provisional government and set about uniting the Métis and their Plains Indian neighbours. The Northwest Rebellion had started, sparked by raids and skirmishes between government forces and the Métis and First Nations. It culminated in the Battle of Batoche, where the army defeated the Métis led by Riel and Dumont. Riel was tried in Regina, found guilty of treason, and, despite the jury's request for clemency, hanged in Regina on November 16, 1885.

TEN THINGS YOU MIGHT NOT KNOW ABOUT LOUIS RIEL

1. He initially studied for the priesthood in Montreal but switched to law.
2. He was pardoned for Scott's execution in 1875 but ordered to stay out of the country for five years.
3. Riel was a U.S. citizen and a teacher when Dumont contacted him in Montana in 1884.
4. One night during his journey from Montana back to Saskatchewan, Riel dreamed of the gallows.
5. In 1875 Riel had a private audience with U.S. president Ulysses S. Grant.
6. Whereas the Métis had a lot of time before the military reached them in Red River in 1870, the new rail line swiftly brought soldiers to Saskatchewan in 1885.
7. By 1885 Riel believed that God was directing him to lead his people and called himself "Prophet of the New World."
8. During his trial, Riel clashed with his defence team, rejecting their efforts to win his acquittal by proving that he was insane.
9. Public pressure, primarily in Quebec, persuaded Ottawa to delay the execution in order to assess Riel's mental state. One of the three examining doctors decided that Riel was in fact insane, but that divergent opinion was never reflected in the final report, and the federal cabinet approved the execution.
10. Riel's body was disguised when it was transported to Manitoba for burial in order to avoid any problems.

In 1998, Winnipeg lawyer Ronald Olesky unearthed some interesting information that casts doubt on the propriety of Riel's conviction. It suggests that Manitoba chief justice Lewis Wallbridge shouldn't have sat on an appeal panel hearing Riel's case because he had earlier provided advice on how to convict the man.

Riel's right-hand man was Gabriel Dumont, a Métis every bit as colourful as his boss, if a bit less controversial. Dumont was born in Red River, Manitoba, in 1838. In 1884 he joined the delegation of Saskatchewan Métis who travelled to St. Peter's, Montana, to invite Riel to lead them once again. Dumont became Riel's military leader and won the battles of Duck Lake and Fish Creek. When the rebellion came to a head in Batoche, Dumont led the Métis defence for four days.

John Diefenbaker called Gabriel Dumont "the greatest Indian fighter of all time, a man beside whom Buffalo Bill was a novice." As a boy growing up in Saskatchewan, the future prime minister met the former Métis military commander. Dief claimed that he saw Dumont, well into his 70s, throw a tin can in the air and shoot it twice before it hit the ground.

Dumont came to a happier end than Riel. After the rebellion failed, he fled to the United States and worked for a time in Buffalo Bill's famed Wild West Show. He died at Batoche in 1906.

Who Was Big Bear?

No fan of the treaties, for sure. Like many Indian leaders, he recognized the adverse way that European settlement would affect the traditional way of life. He proved prescient.

Gimli son Leo Kristjanson was the sixth president of the University of Saskatchewan.

Big Bear (Mistahimaskwa) was a short, thin man whose physical appearance hardly suggested the influence that he wielded among his people and other Plains Indians. Along with Little Pine and Piapot — also Cree chiefs — Big Bear refused to sign the treaties. They moved their people to the Cypress Hills in search of food. In 1870 Big Bear resided in Montana and met with Riel as well as Crowfoot, chief of the Blackfoot, old foes of the Cree. Big Bear's resistance was ill-timed: the disappearance of the buffalo crippled the Natives' ability to survive according to their traditional practices over the centuries. His people were starving, but the Canadian government wouldn't provide food for First Nations not covered by a treaty. Big Bear had little choice but to sign Treaty 8 on December 8, 1882, but he still dreamed of uniting the Plains Indians and forming a confederacy that would force Ottawa to renegotiate treaties that seemed unfair or were not being honoured. In 1884 he convened an enormous Sun Dance near Battleford and invited the chiefs of the Plains tribes to attend to discuss the plan. At a subsequent council meeting at Duck Lake, one of the people in attendance was Louis Riel. During the Riel-led Métis rebellion of 1885, Big Bear and Poundmaker (a Stoney associated through his mother's family with a Cree band near Battleford and the adopted son of Blackfoot chief Crowfoot) rebelled

35

against white rule and tried to form a Cree alliance, one that they hoped would exist within a self-governed area, unhindered by the restrictions found on the reserves.

Big Bear confessed that he was losing control of his people to younger, more militant men. One of them was his own son, Ayimisis, or Little Bad Man. On April 2, 1885, in one of the formative incidents of the Northwest Rebellion, Little Bad Man and Wandering Spirit, Big Bear's war chief, led an attack on the Frog Lake settlement, killing nine settlers. They torched Fort Pitt and fought the Canadian army before being defeated at Loon Lake. Poundmaker's warriors looted food from several abandoned settlers' homes near Fort Battleford, fuelling the settlers' hysteria about a violent Indian uprising. In an ensuing battle, Poundmaker's forces defeated soldiers led by Lieutenant Colonel W. D. Otter at Cut Knife Hill.

Poundmaker and Big Bear surrendered in May and July respectively. Big Bear had argued for a negotiated resolution to his people's concerns and had even protected white survivors of the Frog Lake attack. Poundmaker had also demonstrated restraint, commanding his warriors at the close of the Cut Knife Hill battle not to kill any more than the eight soldiers who had already fallen. Both men were nonetheless arrested following their surrender. They were tried and convicted of treason. They escaped Riel's fate, though barely. Imprisoned in Stony Mountain Penitentiary, they were released before their terms expired. Poundmaker died in 1886, and Big Bear died two years later.

Gordon Tootoosis, the actor who played Big Bear in a 1998 CBC miniseries, was born on the Poundmaker Reserve — where Big Bear died.

The Wild, Wild West

A young Native led North West Mounted Police on a year-and-a-half-long chase and killed three officers before meeting a violent end himself. Sadly it grew out of a misunderstanding. Almighty Voice, a Plains Cree from the One Arrow Reserve near Batoche, was arrested for stealing a steer during the tough autumn of 1895. His Mountie jailer taunted him with warnings that he would hang for the crime. The 19-year-old thief believed him. That night, Almighty Voice snatched the cell keys through the bars and escaped from the Duck Lake jail. He grabbed his young wife and headed into the bush. A week later, an NWMP sergeant tracking the fugitive found him hunting game. By all accounts, Sergeant C. C. Colebrook tried to arrest his quarry peacefully, but Almighty Voice turned and shot him through the neck.

For two years, Almighty Voice and his wife remained at large while Prairie newspapers used his exploits to heighten anti-Native fears. The NWMP eventually tracked him, his cousin, and his brother-in-law to a poplar bluff near Batoche in 1897. In the ensuing and prolonged gunfight, Almighty Voice and his two teenaged accomplices killed two Mounties and one postmaster. The police response was decisive. More than 100 men and two cannons shot at the fugitives for four hours, killing all three.

To soften the ride, buffalo hide covered the wheels of the Red River cart.

One gunslinger who broke laws south of the border was pretty much just another guy when he took a job as a cowboy at Alberta's Bar U Ranch in 1890. Harry Longabaugh was none other than the Sundance Kid, the most infamous member of Butch Cassidy's gang of bank robbers. He headed north to escape the law's tightening net and found work at several ranches, all of which were no doubt happy to have this skilled horseman and, by all accounts, gentleman. The Sundance Kid even became part owner of a Calgary hotel in 1891, but he moved back to the United States the following year. Once there, he reverted to dishonest work and reportedly met his death following a robbery in Bolivia in 1908.

The Sundance Kid's partner, Butch Cassidy, covered a lot of terrain as he tried to keep ahead of the law. The northernmost point in his travels was the odd, lunarlike landscape of the Big Muddy Badlands south of Moose Jaw. The walls and valleys offer about as many hiding spots as you're going to find in this otherwise low-key terrain.

Q: IF IT'S 5:30 IN REGINA, WHAT TIME IS IT IN MOOSE JAW?
A: *1952.*
That's my favourite small-town joke. Moose Javians probably tell a variation that makes fun of Swift Current. However, the Jaw is no typical small city. For many years, its red lights shone redder than those of any other city. Local folklore maintains that famed Chicago gangster Al Capone visited often. He and other bootleggers used the city's notorious system of underground tunnels to elude the police (who didn't really look that hard). Chinese immigrants built

the first tunnels in the 1890s. They literally lived underground, working and saving enough money until they could pay the federal "head tax" on Chinese immigrants. The tunnels link the CPR station to buildings along Main and River Streets. They came in handy whenever police raided brothels and gambling dens: patrons scampered out through the subterranean exits. In fact, the police usually gave the citizens plenty of time to make their getaway. In 1996 this colourful netherworld changed from times past to pastime with the introduction of public walking tours.

After Sitting Bull kicked Custer's butt at Little Bighorn, he wisely moved to a safer locale. To escape recriminations from the U.S. cavalry, the Sioux chief led his people to the Cypress Hills in southwestern Saskatchewan in 1877. The North West Mounted Police sent in Superintendent James Walsh to advise the Sioux of their new host's laws. The chief and the Mountie became friends, and the Sioux remained in Canada until 1881, when a nervous Ottawa refused to give supplies to Sitting Bull's people. The chief moved them to Fort Qu'Appelle, but they were not welcome there, and they finally returned to the United States. Sitting Bull was arrested and spent two years in jail. After all that drama and tragedy, he ended his days as a live exhibit in Buffalo Bill Cody's Wild West Show.

The Melting Pot

For tens of thousands of people seeking a better existence around the turn of the century, the Canadian plains were a back-breaking gamble but a vast improvement over what they were leaving. The massive influx of people from all across Europe created a unique situation in which groups of people who had little in common were all living a similar adventure. This mixing of cultures was responsible for much of how the Prairies have turned out. Our foods, religions, traditions, and arts are all rooted in nations an ocean away. It wasn't until well into the 20th century that the number of Prairie inhabitants who were born here actually outnumbered those who had crossed an ocean to get here.

For Example ...

The most prominent group of immigrants, in number and influence, was the Ukrainians. More than that of any other ethnic group, their culture remains vibrant and easily identifiable. Indeed, any discussion of Prairie food begins with "perogies."

From 1897 to 1912, 594,000 people left the Ukraine for Canada. Circumstances were favourable for "the men in sheepskin coats" to adjust to life here. Winter in the Ukraine wasn't as prolonged or as cold as it was here, but it did include heavy snowfalls and frigid temperatures. And the old country's soil had already made wheat farmers of many families.

The first Ukrainians arrived in Alberta in 1892, but far more would follow. During a subsequent land shortage in the Ukraine, Dr. Joseph Oleskew was assigned the task of looking for a new home, and in 1895 he wrote to the Canadian government. The doctor was clearly a shrewd shopper. He mentioned in his letter that the Brazilian government had recently made overtures to attract his restless people.

Oleskew visited Canada that year and was impressed by the opportunities, the railway network, and the government's offer of land. He conveyed those and other impressions to his countryfolk. I don't know how many Ukrainians ever emigrated to Brazil, but it's fair to say that Canada won this particular PR campaign.

Minister of Immigration Clifford Sifton, who touted the Prairies to the rest of the world, spoke of Ukrainians admiringly if a bit patronizingly: "A stalwart peasant in a sheepskin coat, born on the soil, whose forefathers have been farmers for ten generations, with a stout wife, and a half dozen children, is good quality, as an immigrant."

Between 1901 and 1913, 188,000 emigrants left England for new lives settling the Prairies.

Re-Creating Communities

One hundred German-speaking families left Eastern Galicia within the Austro-Hungarian empire in 1889. They settled on farmland surrounding Medicine Hat. This exemplifies a recurring theme in the settlement of the Prairies. Immigrants from one country moved to a common location where they could live together and keep their culture alive. In 1894 another German exodus brought families from the Ukraine to the Edmonton region, where they formed the towns of Bruderheim and Bruderfeld. By the turn of the century, they were Alberta's third-largest ethnic group, after the British and Plains Indians.

In differing numbers, settlers poured into western Canada from Poland, Hungary, Austria, Romania, and Czechoslovakia between the 1880s and the start of World War I. The twin forces of an inhospitable homeland and the promise of owning land fuelled the migration.

Four hundred Icelanders moved to Canada in 1874. Their leader, Sigtryggur Jonasson, chose a site on the western shore of Lake Winnipeg, 90 kilometres north of Winnipeg, where they could create a single community. They named it Gimli, which sounds more impressive when translated into English as "paradise." Actually Gimli was their second choice: the first suggestion was the rather optimistic Republic of New Iceland. They encountered plenty of problems adjusting. Lake fish swam right through the holes of the nets that they had brought with them. Many families didn't build their homes before the first blizzard hit and spent that first winter inside tents borrowed from the Hudson's Bay Company. A smallpox epidemic in 1876 cut through the population. The settlers hung in there, overcame those obstacles, and developed Manitoba's freshwater fishing industry. Gimli still has a fishing fleet, but it has also grown into one of the province's loveliest tourist towns.

Jeanne-Mathilde Sauvé, Canada's first female governor general, was born in Prud'homme, Saskatchewan.

The Mennonites who settled west of the Red River between 1874 and 1879 simply traded one prairie for another. The Protestant group had long farmed the plains of Russia. They emigrated to escape the Russian government's insistence that they serve in the military, an occupation that ran counter to one of the basic rules of their faith. The Mennonites brought cooperative grain farming with them. They lived in villages and divided the surrounding farmland equally between the various households. Within a few years, they had transformed wild grasslands into arable fields. For a region so dependent on agriculture, the Prairies have seemingly glossed over the Mennonites' contributions to our way of life. In short, they were the first to prove that it could be done.

The Most Unusual Colony of All

Surely it was Cannington Manor. When it was formed in the 1880s, the first upper-class families arrived with dinner jackets, cricket bats, and a servant or two. They came to Moose Mountain in southeastern Saskatchewan to create a truly British colony, one that compromised little to its new surroundings. They raised thoroughbred horses and even built a track to race them. The Cannington Manor Hunt Club held fox hunts, with the participants adorned in the traditional red hunting jackets and knee-high boots. The foxes, like the manor inhabitants themselves, were imported from England.

Certainly these settlers' experience of "breaking the west" was unlike that of the other European groups who came here to work the soil. The Cannington crew were not farmers by nature. Instead, they built a respected flour mill. In 1885 their flour won a gold medal at the World's Fair in Paris. However, few of the families stuck it out. They found other homes in the new land or moved back to England.

Not Our Finest Moment

Prior to the Japanese air attack on Pearl Harbor in 1941, there were only 534 people of Japanese ancestry living in Alberta. Japanese settlement in Canada was almost exclusively centred on the B.C. coastline. The war in the Pacific brought long-held anti-Japanese feelings to a head and prompted Ottawa to invoke the War Measures Act. Japanese-Canadian families were rounded up and sent to internment camps for the remainder of the hostilities. Some opted for life as labourers in the beet fields of Alberta and Manitoba. By war's end, Alberta's Japanese-Canadian population had grown to 3,650. For several years after, Japanese Canadians suffered outright hostility. Lethbridge, a city that once invoked anti-Japanese bylaws, today exhibits a distinct Japanese-Canadian presence. It is home to the Nikka Yuko Centennial Garden, a genuine re-creation of a Japanese garden and a sensible spot to stop while passing through: its calm, graceful beauty is an ideal tonic after hours of highway driving.

The Deal

Under the Homestead Act, a settler was given a parcel of land. He had to build a home on it and clear at least four hectares a year for three years. If he did that — and actually maintained his residence on the property for at least six months a year — he was given clear title after the three years.

The first settlers literally broke the land. They had to chop, hoe, and yank out much brush to clear space for their homesteads. They walked up and down the expanse of arable grasslands, turning the ground with a single-blade walking plow. An animal-driven plow was a luxury. This practice gave birth to the term "sodbuster."

41

Before Electricity

- No one could have guessed how important journalism would be to the lives of the settlers. First, it opened up windows on the world that they had left behind, alleviating some of the isolation they must have felt. Second, it actually filled the cracks around the drafty windows in their homes: old copies of newspapers were pasted to the walls to cover cracks and provide some protection from the cold.
- Farm families short on coal could always use buffalo chips for fuel. The dried and hardened dung didn't lend itself to romantic scenes in front of the fire, but it kept people warm.
- In the beginning, laundry was a minimal affair. Soap, a bucket of water, and some really dirty clothes. The water, often collected from a standing slough, wasn't exactly an ideal cleaning agent.
- With no refrigeration, early settlers used a brine barrel to store pork. Hogs were butchered in cool weather, and the meat was rubbed with a salt-sugar mixture to draw out the blood. (For some reason, the mixture included salt-petre, which is probably why pork doesn't enjoy a reputation as an aphrodisiac today.) The next day, the meat was stuffed into a barrel containing a brine made of water, sugar, and salt, where it remained until it was eaten.
- The smokehouse was another method of keeping meat edible. The key was in creating a fire that produced enough smoke to dry and flavour the meat but not enough heat to cook it.

Those Dirty, Dirty Thirties

During the Dirty Thirties, nature compounded the nation's political and economic problems. A prolonged drought eroded soil and created sandstorms throughout the southern section of the Prairies shared by Alberta and Saskatchewan. The result was termed "the Dust Bowl."

DEPRESSING RETURNS

The downward cycle of the Depression soon enveloped wheat, dairy, and live-stock prices. Wheat fell to its lowest price in 300 years when no. 1 Northern grade went for under 39.5 cents per bushel in December 1932. The net return to the farmer worked out to 20 cents. Eggs went wholesale at three cents a dozen, and 45 kilograms of beef only brought in three bucks.

TALES FROM TOUGH TIMES

Marie Hoffman was challenged time and again as a Prairie pioneer, but never so much as during her years trying to make a living off an uncooperative land-scape during the 1930s. She remembers the Bennett buggies, government relief, and having to pack wet cloths into the boards of the house to shut out the sandstorms.

Marie was six years old when her family travelled by ship from Russia to Canada in 1914. Her father was a Mennonite preacher who brought them to Hepburn, Saskatchewan, near Saskatoon, and then to a farm outside Maple Creek. She married in 1928, but her husband died within three years, so Marie took a job at a nearby ranch. Matchmakers introduced her to Mr. Hoffman, a widower with three children. They married and had three more children.

From 1932 to 1940, when they moved to Medicine Hat, the Hoffmans worked the land. Or tried to. There just wasn't that much to work with. They were poor, but so was most everyone else, Marie says.

These days, she's an astoundingly sharp 90-something who wheels her-self around the halls of a nursing home in Medicine Hat. When she starts talk-ing about those days, her memory sharpens before your eyes, and one story leads to another. Here are two that capture life in that dirty decade.

One cold day, Marie's husband and his brother went in search of coal. By day's end, they had filled their horse-drawn cart with the black fuel. Too late to venture home, they lay down under the stars.

"In the morning when they got up, somebody had stolen the coal and cut the reins on the horse," Marie says. "They had to spend time finding the horse."

The men returned home with the horse but no coal and explained their predicament to their wives. Marie and her sister-in-law bundled up their chil-dren and went in search of the local RCMP officer. They found him inside his well-heated home.

The Mountie was authorized to sign vouchers that people could take to a merchant to exchange for goods. It was a makeshift social program at a time when pride was a luxury. After listening to their story, the constable decided that it didn't warrant a voucher. He wasn't about to sign a chit that the women could exchange for coal.

"We said to him, 'We brought our kids along, and we intend to stay in your house, which is so nice and warm.'" The Mountie sized up the women and the children. "He wrote a receipt pretty fast," Marie says.

Families stretched each dollar as if it were made of taffy. One of Marie's daughters once swallowed a tack that had been embedded in the lining of her carriage. The pointy intruder lodged in the-three-year old's bronchial tube, so mother and child set off to Calgary for the necessary surgical exorcism. Marie had three dollars for the entire trip. She spent the first buck getting them there. "With 25 cents, I bought her a little doll to hold when she went to hospital," Marie says. The procedure and recovery took three days, during which time Marie stayed at the YWCA.

**Gabriel Dumont was reportedly buried standing up ...
so that he could see the enemy coming.**

When it was time to return home, a man from the welfare office accompanied Marie and her daughter to the train station. When Marie handed him a quarter and asked him to buy them a few cookies for the trip back, he gave it back to her. "He went and bought us a whole bag full of cookies, with his own money." Mother and child reached Medicine Hat by rail and then hitched a ride in a truck back to their farm. Marie remembers when the truck pulled up in front of their home and Mr. Hoffman came out to greet them. "He was going to pay the man, and I said, 'No, I still have one dollar.' That's what you could do with three dollars at that time."

Help from Above

The people who settled this land brought not only strong backs but also strong faiths. Religion directly forged some communities as people of minority faiths banded together to worship in peace (which many had been denied in the countries that they had left behind). It also provided solace to many a farmer set upon by a multitude of challenges and hardships. Ottawa promised quarter-sections of farmland to families who broke the land, but settlers willing to establish communities of 20 or more families were allowed to take on bigger tracts. Ottawa set aside the homestead residency requirements and permitted Mennonite families to reside in hamlets, in accordance with their beliefs.

Religion shaped education as those communities set up their own schools. Catholic and Anglican missionaries controlled Indian education until the 1950s. Unfortunately the missionaries failed to perceive that the Plains Indians already had a highly evolved belief system, one that didn't need to be replaced. Suppression of their religious practices culminated in the 1895 ban on the Sun Dance ceremony. The famous Barr colony established near Lloydminster at the turn of the century grew out of an idealistic plan to create

44

a prosperous Anglican English community. Religion repeatedly affected politics: many Jews allied themselves with the Independent Labour Party, the One Big Union, the Co-operative Commonwealth Federation, and the New Democratic Party. In 1926 A. A. Heaps became the first Jew from the Prairies to sit in the House of Commons.

The first religion on the Prairies came with the first people. The medicine bundle was an important spiritual possession for a Plains Indian. It could be feathers, sweetgrass, rocks, or ceremonial items such as paint and pipes, wrapped in a cloth or cinched within a leather bag. The contents were anything but random: each item signified an event or vision, and the bag's owner was expected to learn a chant for each object. Because each bundle was considered powerful, the people traded between themselves to obtain a bundle, and the price was always high. The transfer of ownership was marked by a ceremony.

The Sun Dance was the most cherished and important ritual in the lives of the Plains people. The three-day festival drew them together from a large area. The hunters searched for a tree to be used as the central pole in the Sun Dance lodge and stalked it like an enemy before chopping it down. Once the lodge was built, the people attached offerings to the pole and the rafters. The first day of the ceremony was reserved for ritual dances, with the third day set aside for a magnificent feast. Nearly every Plains tribe practised some variation on the Sun Dance. The most dramatic event involved skewering the skin of young men with hooks attached to a pole around which they danced and prayed, tearing their flesh as a sign of their faith.

The fur trade is central to the history of The Pas and explains why this northern Manitoba community is home to Métis, First Nations, and people of European ancestry. This cultural stew is reflected by Christ Church. It was built by Henry Budd, who was ordained in 1853 and became the first Aboriginal Anglican priest in western Canada. One wall of the church is decorated by the Ten Commandments and the Lord's Prayer — written in Cree.

In 1855 Sister Ste. Therese was sent from Quebec to Grantown, the agrarian Métis community west of Fort Garry. Her manner and her medical skills won over the town, so much so that the residents were heartbroken when they learned three years later that the Catholic Church was assigning her back to Quebec. No amount of pleading could change the plan. Keeping Sister Ste. Therese was going to take something more. On the appointed day, the sister and another nun were placed in armchairs atop a Red River cart and driven out of town. As they passed through a wooded area, half a dozen Sioux attacked the cart. The men grabbed the chair on which Sister Ste. Therese was sitting and loaded it into a waiting cart — careful to handle only her chair for fear that touching a nun would mean excommunication. She didn't protest much, having recognized the "Sioux" as several of the Grantown Métis. They "kidnapped" her and headed back to Grantown. This act convinced the church of her importance to the community, and she was permitted to stay on. She later founded St. Boniface Hospital and St. Mary's Academy.

Former Manitoba premier John Norquay had a reputation as an enthusiastic dancer.

The first mosque in North America was built in Edmonton in 1938, thanks to the 34 Muslims living there at the time.

Shaarey Zedek ("Gates of Justice") was the first synagogue on the Prairies, built in Winnipeg in 1888.

At just 3.5 x 2 metres, Canada's smallest church is the chapel built in the Valley of the Dinosaurs near Drumheller, Alberta.

On the Move!

The introduction of the horse to North America drastically changed the way of life of the Plains Indians in the 18th century. The Blackfoot used family dogs to carry tipis and other possessions in devices called travois. When it was time to move, the family disassembled the tipi and strapped the hide cover between two of the long poles, like a hammock. The other ends of the poles were harnessed to the dog. Each dog travois was only good for carrying about 30 kilograms. When the horse arrived, the poles of a much larger travois could be lashed to the sides of this much bigger animal. As a result, families could erect larger tipis and own more possessions.

The Red River cart didn't need a horn or even an engine to make noise. The croaking of its ungreased wooden axle was more than sufficient to signal its approach. However, it could have used shock absorbers. This was the first minivan: an ox-drawn cart balanced on two wooden wheels, each measuring two metres across. Wooden pegs and strips of rawhide held its components in place. It first appeared in 1801 and would later become a common sight around the Red River Colony. When many families moved at once, they formed a convoy of carts, squawking their way across the prairie. When they encountered a river, they removed the wheels and floated the boxy passenger compartment downstream like a raft.

As the carts traversed popular routes, they cut paths into the soil. Years later, many of those trails became paved roads. Now that provincial budgets have reduced spending on highway maintenance, it's possible to drive the same roads and experience exactly what our ancestors felt when they travelled by Red River cart.

The phrase "prairie schooner" is evocative. It refers to the covered wagons that brought settlers to the Plains. The maritime allusion is fitting if one imagines the pale canvases rolling steadily forward on a sea of grass.

Bull trains were the precursor to the commercial trucking industry. As many as 10 pairs of oxen would pull three linked wagons loaded with food, supplies, and other consumer goods. The wagons covered about 16 kilometres of road a day. In an example of clear, accurate terminology, the whip-toting drivers were called bullwhackers.

The Riverboats

There are no tales of gamblers, no Frankie and Johnny, and certainly no Huck and Jim. Yet Mississippi-style steamboats once navigated Prairie rivers. The paddle-wheel steamboat in use in the United States since 1787 first appeared on the Red River in 1859. Those who could afford first class were treated to fine dining and tinkling piano music. Steamers carried the first wheat exported from Manitoba and, unwitting participants in their own demise, transported the first locomotive engine to Winnipeg for the CPR.

The first steamer west of the Red River was the *Baroness*, built in 1883 in Lethbridge (then known as Coal Banks) by the North West Coal and Navigation Company. Between 1883 and 1908, up to 15 stern-wheelers hauled people and cargo along the North and South Saskatchewan Rivers during the months between spring thaw and winter freeze-up. The pilots were often seamen who had come west to homestead, mistakenly believing their maritime days to be behind them. Medicine Hat actually hosted a successful boatyard during this period.

One steamer, the *Northcote*, played what turned out to be a fairly ineffective role in the Northwest Rebellion of 1885. Major General Frederick Middleton, commander of the Canadian militia, ordered that the boat be loaded with soldiers and supplies and brought upriver from its dock in Medicine Hat to Battleford. Due to low water, the four-day journey turned into one of 14 days, with lengthy stops each time the vessel ran aground. The boat's second duty was to serve as a floating fortress at the Battle of Batoche from which soldiers could fire at the Métis while Middleton's men stormed the rebels on land. But none of his men ran as quickly as the river's current: the *Northcote* beat them to Batoche, came under much fire, and was rendered useless when the Métis lowered a ferry cable that sheared off its smokestack.

The *City of Medicine Hat* was only a few years old when it embarked on a pleasure cruise from the Hat to Saskatoon on May 29, 1908. Except for the last kilometre or so, the 640-kilometre journey was uneventful. Spring runoff had boosted water levels along the South Saskatchewan, so much so that the steamer was too tall to pass under the city's several bridges. The captain ordered the smokestack removed, and the steamer cleared the first two bridges. Before it reached the third, telephone wires spanning the river caught on the boat and ensnared the steering apparatus. The boat crashed into the pillars supporting the third bridge and rolled over on its side. No one was injured, but the uncompleted journey was ominous: the steamer's passengers returned home by rail, the new mode of transportation that proved faster, more dependable, and more popular. *The City of Medicine Hat*'s failed voyage proved to be the last attempt to navigate the South Saskatchewan by steamboat.

Earlier this century, transportation on the Prairies took a giant step backward. The Bennett buggy first appeared during the Depression and was named after the not-fondly remembered Calgary lawyer who led the country from 1930 to 1935. Unable to maintain their vehicles during the Depression, farmers yanked out the engines and hitched the front bumpers to teams of horses. We're nothing if not pragmatic. The Anderson cart appeared around the same time. Named after Alberta's premier at the time, it was really a stripped-down car chassis tied to a horse team.

A more recent Prairie road warrior turned up in the 1960s. Premier Ross Thatcher allowed Saskatchewan's pickup trucks to be regarded as farm vehicles, thereby qualifying to use gasoline that was taxed less heavily and therefore cheaper. To take advantage of this saving, some enterprising drivers turned their cars into pseudotrucks by cutting away the backs. The result was called a Thatcher wagon.

Narcisse, Manitoba, is home to the world's largest collection of wriggling red-sided garter snakes. Tens of thousands squirm together in dens and emerge for three weeks each spring to mate, drawing spectators from around the world.

Prairie Patriots

THE CHIEF
In 1957 John George Diefenbaker ended 22 years of Liberal rule by becoming prime minister. The leader of the Progressive Conservatives was born in Ontario but grew up in Prince Albert, Saskatchewan. Diefenbaker opened up grain sales to the People's Republic of China and attacked South African apartheid as early as 1961. He lost power in 1963 and lost the Tory leadership in 1967. He died in 1979.

Despite a rumpled, mush-mouthed persona, his most potent weapon was his sharp wit, one that Diefenbaker wielded against many a political opponent. Some Diefisms:

- "It was so dry in Saskatchewan during the Depression that the trees were chasing the dogs."
- "Those were the days when the only protection a Conservative enjoyed in the province of Saskatchewan was under the provisions of the game laws." (April 29, 1966)
- "It is interesting that an appointment to it (the Senate) seems to be a tremendous encouragement to longevity." (April 26, 1965)
- "I've got all my enemies in the cabinet, where I can keep an eye on them." (March 14, 1959)

BIBLE BILL
It's not hard to understand William Aberhart's nickname. Aberhart looked heavenward for inspiration and direction. Many Albertans looked to him in

the same way. The radio evangelist stands alongside John Diefenbaker and Tommy Douglas as one of the great Prairie populists. In 1935 Aberhart became leader of the first Social Credit government in the country when he was elected premier of Alberta, a position that he held until his death in 1943. His party took 56 of 63 seats by promising, among other things, a payment of $25 per month — dubbed "funny money" — to Albertans. The federal government quashed this and other election promises as being outside his jurisdiction. However, Aberhart's stand against debt collection saved many Albertans from losing their homes and farms.

Government House in Regina is said to be haunted by "Howie," a cook who died there in 1938.

Aberhart had a hand in one of Alberta's most offbeat political campaigns. He helped to write the *Man from Mars* radio series broadcast in late 1934 and early 1935. It featured an extraterrestrial who, each episode, encountered yet another case of Liberal mismanagement. Although not technically a registered voter in this part of the solar system, the visitor made it clear that he supported Social Credit.

THE FATHER OF MEDICARE
The role of Tommy Douglas in the introduction of medicare — the feat for which he remains best known — was chronicled a few pages back. Most everything that this charismatic little man did stemmed from a social conscience deeply impacted during the 1930s, when he sought to comfort people as a Baptist preacher in Weyburn, Saskatchewan. He was drawn into politics and won a seat for the Co-operative Commonwealth Federation in the 1935 federal election. He returned to provincial politics and in 1944 established the first socialist government in North America. He remained premier until 1961, when he quit to lead the CCF's successor, the New Democratic Party, a position that he held for 10 years.

Looking back, it's not hard to figure out why Douglas led so successfully and is still so fondly remembered. He was very much a man of the people, and it wasn't an act. His résumé includes two activities that ought to be mandatory for any politician: comic after-dinner speaking, and amateur boxing.

50

Chapter 3

Where We Live, How We Live

DARLENE HAY: WHERE THE WILD THINGS ARE

Nearly everyone has seen the Typical Prairie Painting. There is a grain elevator. The sun is setting. The parallel steel spines of a rail line recede into the distance and converge. A dirt road runs across the front of the frame, but there are no vehicles, except maybe a long-dead pickup parked in grille-high grass. Overhead, geese form a flapping arrowhead aimed at some warmer destination. Saskatchewan's gift shops and galleries are full of such images. They reinforce an entrenched misconception: that there's nothing more to the Prairies than agriculture and endless horizons.

Saskatoon artist Darlene Hay paints the Prairies too, although anyone who sees her work might be forgiven for not realizing it. Her paintings don't look like the Prairies at all.

Hay has been painting for 27 years. An original farmgirl, she studied art at Saskatchewan's two universities and participated in the Emma Lake workshops, a famed series of educational retreats for artists, dating back to the 1950s. Not surprisingly the avid bird-watcher's first paintings were landscapes. Then Darlene got her hands on a binocular microscope and painted magnified plant forms in precise detail. She moved on to abstract painting and eventually returned to landscapes. And this time they were informed by all that she had done before, including the more dramatic use of colour and a looser visual style.

In 1993 Darlene approached Nature Saskatchewan and Canada Trust-Friends of the Environment for grant money to promote a series of large canvases called Save Our Endangered Spaces. The project ended up as a chronicle of her travels to little-known ecological treasures around Saskatchewan. Everywhere she went in search of examples of fragile beauty, she encountered reminders of how vulnerable that beauty is. At Clearwater River, north of La Loche, her view of the northern boreal forest was disrupted by the ominous sight of a forest industry representative measuring the width of the trees.

"I'm not down on oil exploration or logging, but there needs to be a place for the wild as well," she says. "There's a wild beauty about the Prairies I don't want to see go. We still have it. You have to look for it, but it's still there."

Sometimes you don't have to look that hard. During one of her excursions, as she sat in front of the canvas that she had hauled into the wild, Darlene heard a noise behind her. Two deer were watching her, perhaps wondering why someone would want to paint their home.

As Darlene drove along back roads, walked across open fields, and sauntered along wooded trails — her paints and canvases usually in tow — she made one discovery after another. "The Athabasca sand dunes is one of the real surprises for me," she says. "It was desert from horizon to horizon. There were huge dunes ... four storeys high that you could climb up." So we could film the sequel to *The English Patient* here. Apparently we could also remake *The Poseidon Adventure*. Darlene swears that she's seen deep-sea whitecaps from the vantage point of a tiny boat in the middle of Lake Athabaska. "The waves get to be 50 feet high."

The artist admits that the year-long series of field trips opened her eyes. "Before I went on this adventure, I guess I would have concentrated on the open spaces. The wheat fields. But there are pockets of these very wild, wilderness-type areas that are virtually untouched by man. They are in real danger of going, and going very quickly."

There's a catch-22 here. The relative obscurity of the natural diversity on the Prairies has saved these wild spaces from being literally trampled underfoot by tourists and residents alike. But that lack of familiarity also makes it harder to convince people to lobby for protection of these places.

Darlene supports a managed type of tourism that would raise the profiles of these areas without exposing them to overuse. "People will spend oodles of money going across the border to the States or into B.C., thinking that's where you have to go to appreciate nature." The key, according to her, is to stop the car. Pull over to the side of the road. Turn the engine off. Go for a walk. "People drive by places, and that's it. It's when you walk through these places that you'll see what's there."

For Hay, the land isn't just an important component of how she earns a living. Take her brushes away and she's still got her binoculars and her bird-watching. Standing knee-deep in wild grass is familiar to her. Comforting. "It's a place to kind of get yourself together. There are so many things coming at you in life. When I get out in nature, there's such a calming. It helps put things in perspective for me. This is where the important things are."

The Land

Just as many Americans believe that the snow, which supposedly starts right at the Canadian border, is lined with the tracks from our dogsleds, many Canadians believe that the Prairies comprise a flat vista of grass and grain fields from the Rockies to the Canadian Shield. There are dozens of places that they could visit to dispel that notion. One of them is Spruce Woods Provincial Park in western Manitoba. For 25 square kilometres, sand dunes rise and fall, offering shelter to the western hognose snake, the northern prairie skink, and two species of cacti.

If our sky is a big-screen TV, then one of the specialty channels that we enjoy is the aurora borealis. I saw the northern lights shimmering and dancing in the sky my first night in Regina, one late-summer evening in 1988. Perhaps because many of our communities are within 160 kilometres of the U.S. border, we think of ourselves as being located firmly in *southern* Canada. The unique and eerie beauty of the aurora borealis reminds us that we inhabit a northern land. The Plains Indians believed that the lights were the spirits of the dead dancing for the Great Spirit.

For those who place faith in science, the northern lights are also attributed to radiation produced by awesome solar storms. The radiation is trapped in the Van Allen belts and directed toward the Earth's north and south poles. The effect, present during magnetic storms and sunspot activity, appears to the eye as sheets of twisting, floating colour.

In April 1997 the Red River rose, raged, and ruined. Ever since Selkirk's settlers built their homes along it, the river has periodically overrun its banks, flooding farmland and homes. The 1997 flood was the worst in 100 years: 28,000 people were evacuated from their homes in the Red River valley. Eight thousand Canadian soldiers were brought in to stack sandbags. Before receding, the water flooded 2,500 homes and caused more than $200 million in damage. Yet it could have been worse. After the devastating flood of 1950, Manitoba premier Duff Roblin approved construction of a costly 47-kilometre concrete depression that reroutes excess water around Winnipeg and dumps it back in the river system north of the city. "Duff's Ditch" wasn't completed until 1968 — but in 1997 it justified all past and future costs. Without it, Portage and Main would have been under three metres of water. We would have ended up with two Lake Winnipegs.

A hoodoo is a column of earth six to nine metres high crowned by a boulder. Erosion shapes the tower but leaves the stone hat on top. Look for hoodoos in the badland valleys of southern Alberta and Saskatchewan.

The lakes and forests of the northern Prairies offer some of the best fishing and hunting in the world, but like any resource this bounty must be respected. In 1937 American hunters realized that drought and farmland were eating up the marshes that North America's waterfowl used for breeding grounds. They formed Ducks Unlimited to raise money to protect Canadian marshlands. The following year, Ducks Unlimited Canada formed in Manitoba and launched its first project, Big Grass Marsh west of Lake Manitoba.

The Great Gopher Hunt was a uniquely Prairie event. During World War I, Saskatchewan's Department of Agriculture engineered a campaign to wipe out the rodents that dug tunnels, tore up fields, and were generally perceived as a threat to farming. Children flooded holes and carried clubs in an effort to collect the bounty of two cents a tail. Schools even encouraged the mercenary pursuit. Students from 980 schools participated in the provincewide Gopher Day on May 1, 1917, when more than half a million gophers were exterminated.

An aerial view of Regina provides surprising evidence of our desire to add that homey touch. The Queen City is thick with trees! And all of them have been hand-planted. An archival photo of the city looks completely different from one taken today. The silhouette of each building is easily distinguishable, rising up from the flat grassland. When the City of Regina — and many homeowners — set out to provide what nature couldn't, they chose to plant elm trees. Of all the shade trees, elms are best because they are most able to survive our extreme winter temperatures.

Five of the 12 UNESCO World Heritage Sites in Canada — Head-Smashed-In Buffalo Jump, Waterton Lakes National Park, the Canadian Rocky Mountain Parks, Wood Buffalo National Park, and Dinosaur Provincial Park — are wholly or partially within Alberta.

The Name Game

What's in a name? Sometimes decades of history, sometimes a winning horse race. Our communities have drawn their names from Native inhabitants, European settlers, monarchs, generals, railway officials, and serendipity. In some cases, the story behind the name has lasted longer than the community itself.

Alberta was not named after Queen Victoria's late husband, Albert. Close, though. The Marquis of Lorne, the governor general of the North-West Territories, dubbed the region Alberta in honour of the queen's fourth daughter, who happened to be his wife. There's a guy who's never stuck for a gift idea.

Gumbo is a rich loam resting on a clay subsoil.

The Cree called the Saskatchewan River *Kisiskatchewani Sipi*, meaning "swift-flowing river." Pioneers shortened the Cree word to *Saskatchewan*, and in 1882 that name was given to the entire district.

Plains Indians also provided the phrase *Manitou bou*. It means "narrows of the Great Spirit" and was named for the thin central point in Lake Manitoba.

ALBERTAN APPELLATIONS

The best-known goofy name in Alberta is **Medicine Hat**. As is often the case, there are a few versions as to how that name came about. The most familiar is that a Cree medicine man lost his hat in the South Saskatchewan River, where the city now sits, during a fight between his people and the Blackfoot. A less colourful version is that a hill east of the city looks a lot like the headpiece of a medicine man. This version is supported somewhat by an 1883 map of the Department of the Interior that cites a hill called Medicine Hat.

Several CPR officials were discussing what to name a little village that sat along the new line that they were building between Calgary and Edmonton. One of the men dropped his pen, which fell nib-first into the map that they were studying. It stuck. So did the name that one of the men suggested: **Penhold**.

Many communities were named in a whimsical, almost arbitrary fashion. Such was the case with the village of **Elnora**. When the villagers met at a home in 1908 to choose a name for their fledgling community, they opted to simply mix the first names of two local women: the hostess, Mrs. *Elinora* Hogg, and Mrs. *Nora* Edwards.

Qu'Appelle is French for "Who calls?" When settlers heard the echoes that ring through the Qu'Appelle Valley, they gave it its name.

A settler named **Hornbeck** couldn't take it when his herd of Percherons died during the winter of 1906. He flipped out, grabbed a gun, and locked himself in a store with four other men. His prisoners finally shot him, an act for which they were tried and acquitted. The hamlet that grew up around the spot assumed the unfortunate horseman's name.

Taber is known for its corn, but its name has nothing to do with agriculture. The name is the first half of "tabernacle" and was picked in tribute to Mormon settlers in the area. If you're wondering what happened to "nacle," then look no farther than nearby **Elcan**, which is "nacle" spelled backward.

First Nations names usually provide descriptions that are simple, accurate, and lovely. Sometimes those names have been anglicized to such an extent that a linguist would be hard-pressed to discern the original meanings. A case in point is **Wetaskiwin**. The Native name was actually *Wi-ta-ski-oo Cha-ka-tin-ow*, or "peace hills."

SASKATCHEWAN SOBRIQUETS

English settlers named **Coronach** after a horse that had won the 1926 Epsom Derby.

Why is **Eastend** in western Saskatchewan? Because the North West Mounted Police built a post there in 1877, at the *eastern* edge of Cypress Hills.

The railway created **Estevan** in 1893. It also inspired the name. It is an amalgamation of CPR executives George *Stephen* and William C. *van* Horne.

Erosion formed the hoodoos. Eventually it will destroy them.

The people of **Mozart** left it to the station agent's wife to name the village. Music was her passion: she also named streets Wagner, Liszt, and Chopin.

The Grand Trunk Pacific Railway settled on a useful formula to name the many small towns that sat along its line through the Prairies. Communities were named alphabetically, A to Z. It ran through the alphabet several times, although X apparently taxed people's imaginations such that it was only used once, at **Xena**, 90 kilometres southeast of Saskatoon.

MANITOBAN MONIKERS

There are several legends behind the naming of the village of **Arden**, northeast of Neepawa. I prefer the tale of the lazy cook. A construction gang working in the area employed a man more interested in sleeping than cooking. His frequent and unscheduled naps prompted the gang foreman to yell "Where's Arden?" over and over again, and the name stuck.

Blood was spilled before **Bull Island** earned its name. Residents of Norway House awoke one morning to find the body of a man named Isbister, who had been fatally gored by a local bull overnight. They shot the bull and transported the creature to a small nearby island. When they burned the carcass, the fire grew beyond their control and burned everything on the island.

Long before *Les Miz* became a musical, a T-shirt, and a desktop calendar, it was a book. *Les Misérables* made Victor Hugo France's best-known author. His fame was international, and the little rail-line community of **Hugo** was named after him.

Killarney's Irish origins are evident in more than its name: it boasts the only green fire engine in Canada. The first settlers called it Oak Lake, but one

57

of them, surveyor John O'Brien, thought that the scenic locale called for something more evocative. The Celtic word translates as "the church among the black thorns."

The early residents of the birthplace of Louis Riel provided a rude shock to Bishop Provencher. On May 18, 1818, he wrote: "It would take the faith of a Boniface to work among these people" — that is, the necessarily rough-and-tumble voyageurs. Boniface was **St. Boniface**, the eighth-century English missionary who became archbishop of the German people. Provencher was inspired by his own comment and named his parish after the long-dead archbishop. The surrounding community — now part of Winnipeg — followed suit.

The Red River is the only river that flows north out of the continental United States.

You might think that if any city were to take its name from a cheap novel called *The Sunless City*, then it would be Vancouver. In fact, it was **Flin Flon**. Prospectors working the Churchill River area found a weathered copy of the 1905 science fiction novel about a gold-laden city in the centre of the Earth. The book's hero was Professor Josiah Flintabbatey Flontin. When a mining community grew up around where the book was found, an abbreviated form of the protagonist's name was used, allowing the good professor to jump mediums, from novel to road map.

Making Tracks

The west wouldn't be what it is today without the rails. More than just an economic necessity for our farmers, a transcontinental railway was integral to John A. Macdonald's vision of a united Canada. The first attempt to build the line crumbled in 1872 when it was discovered that Macdonald had awarded the contract in exchange for campaign donations. When the Conservatives returned to power in 1878, they gave Canadian Pacific Railway a lucrative contract — $25 million and 10 million hectares, for a start — to build the line. The CPR set a course west from Winnipeg to the southern Rockies. Between 1882 and 1885, crews of men worked nonstop, swiftly conquering the flat landscape. It would be another 20 years before Alberta and Saskatchewan would join Canada, but they immediately benefited from the CPR's presence. The rail line was an artery, bringing life to the region.

The CPR route dictated where Prairie towns would be built. Train stations turned into fledgling communities. Speculators bought land along the rail route wherever they thought the CPR might build a station. Those who were right made money; those who guessed wrong often went broke.

Liquor was prohibited among the work crews. As a result, the men had to devise some creative ways to obtain it. They bought hollow "Bibles" made of tin and filled with liquor. One man mailed an organ to the camp, claiming that it was to be used for church services. In fact, it was a hollow container full of booze. It may not have been much use to anyone come Sunday morning, but it was much appreciated the night before.

The Weather: A Prairie Icebreaker

If two Prairie people fell from a high-rise building at the same time, chances are they'd talk about weather on the way down. It's our common winter enemy, the key to our economy, and the reason for our hot, sunny summers. Here are some stats.

- Canada's highest recorded temperature occurred in Midale, Saskatchewan, on July 5, 1937. It reached 45 degrees Celsius. The residents of Gleichen, Alberta, might disagree. Some sources say that the mercury once topped 46 degrees there.
- Medicine Hat enjoys a nation-best average of 271 days a year without precipitation.
- But Estevan is the sunniest community in Canada — 2,537 hours a year.
- On May 30, 1961, more than 25 centimetres of rain fell on Buffalo Gap, Saskatchewan, in less than an hour.
- Of Canada's major cities, Winnipeg suffers through the coldest January: −18.3 degrees Celsius is the average for the month.
- Northeastern Manitoba is the coldest region in the Prairies: temperatures are below −20 degrees Celsius for a third of the year.

Your typical Prairie winter is a lot like your typical trench warfare. After a week of −40 degrees Celsius weather, the mood is surprisingly light-hearted, even gleeful, like the mix of gratitude and disbelief felt by soldiers who somehow survived the bloodiest of battles. But, like those soldiers, our tempers are even more likely to fray when the fighting has simply gone on too long. The same people who survived wind chill in January are apt to whimper at the sight of a light April snowfall. It's not winter's severity that we mind so much as its length. The key to coping is attitude. Winter brings with it an array of recreational opportunities, such as cross-country skiing, skating, or, my favourite, video rental.

Although cabin fever afflicts most everyone, we are generally spared the ravages of seasonal affective disorder — the winter blues. That's because SAD is triggered by a lack of light, not by a lack of warmth. Mild symptoms include fatigue and impaired thinking. At its worst, SAD brings on clinical depression. Luckily the Prairies are blessed with an inordinate amount of sunshine, even in winter. Winnipeg averages 358 hours of sunlight from December to February, compared with 195 hours in Vancouver.

 **Saskatchewan really has a town called Climax and another called Love. Please, folks, if you're going to Climax, then make sure you've been in Love first.**

A two-year-old girl from Rouleau, Saskatchewan, survived the lowest body temperature ever recorded. When Karlee Kosolofski accidentally wandered outside her parents' home early on February 23, 1994, she was trapped outside for six hours at −22 degrees Celsius with a biting wind. Her body temperature fell from 37 to 14 degrees Celsius. When she was found and rushed to hospital in Regina, she had no vital signs. She had frozen to death.

Yet doctors managed to save her life by methodically removing her blood, warming it, and pumping it back into her tiny frame. She remains the only person ever to survive a core body temperature of 14 degrees Celsius. Karlee lost her left leg below the knee to frostbite, but she became a worldwide phenomenon and Saskatchewan's own miracle.

> "I can remember being lost on the prairie one winter night in a blizzard — an experience that time does not eradicate or the passing interval make dim. My Uncle Ed and I had gone to a school concert at Halcyonia that March night in 1909, and it was a three-and-a-half mile sleigh drive home. We left at 10 o'clock, and we could see in the distance the light that my father always used to put out on the door. But the horse could not face the blizzard, and turned off. And so we were lost. We had to spend the night in an open cutter turned up on its side.

We were lucky. The storm broke in the morning, and we were safe.

"Was I fearful of losing my life? Let me say this: it was a frightening experience I would not like to repeat."

— *John Diefenbaker, 1960*

In the Prairies, the phrase "wind chill" is as frightening as "red tide" in British Columbia. It's the demon that we all live with six to eight months a year. Since 1949 we've thrown this phrase around, usually without understanding the labyrinthine formula behind it.

The wind chill index measures the twin effects of temperature and wind speed on the human body. As a number, it reflects the amount of body heat lost (watts per square metre). If it's –20 degrees Celsius, and the wind is blowing at 40 kilometres an hour, then the index reads about 2,000 watts per square metre. The effect on the body is considered the equivalent of –45 degrees Celsius!

How big a role does the wind play in our notorious winters? Think of it this way: the temperature is a sharp knife pointed at your face. The wind is the knife thrower.

Hoar frost. When people first hear a reference to winter's delicate window dressing, they're likely to raise their eyebrows. Granted, standing on a street corner in winter probably does court frostbite, but hoar frost has nothing to do with that trade. It's simply ice crystals forming around thin rounded surfaces, such as tree branches and telephone wires. When you see it, you might think you've walked into a Hallmark Christmas card.

A 290-gram hailstone — Canada's biggest — fell on Cedoux, Saskatchewan, in 1973.

Southwestern Alberta benefits from the warming embrace of chinooks. About 35 a year, in fact. Calgary is the biggest beneficiary, although a few chinooks reach as far east as Medicine Hat. Cool, moist Pacific air rises over the mountains, drops its watery payload as rain or snow, and warms up as it rushes down the eastern side of the Rockies. Within hours, it can raise temperatures by up to 20 degrees Celsius. One more reason for Calgarians to feel pleased with themselves.

The chinook has prompted one oft-repeated fish story. Not long after a prolonged snowfall, a turn-of-the-century rancher reportedly tied his horse to a telegraph pole before he went into a store at Pincher Creek, Alberta. While he was inside, a chinook blew in from the mountains and immediately sent the mercury heavenward. When the man came out, he found his horse still tied to the pole, but its hooves were dangling more than a metre above the ground.

Winter is cold but sunny on the Prairies, blizzards notwithstanding. A frequent phenomenon is the appearance of sundogs — semicircular lights that border the sun. In some cases, they completely encircle it. Once you hear the name, it's hard not to imagine a pair of canines, patiently sitting alongside their master. The sundogs are caused by light reflecting through airborne ice crystals. Some people say that their appearance heralds a winter blizzard.

The Great Escape
One of the most faithful indicators of winter's approach is the sight of nature's creatures beginning the annual flight southward. Each fall, you can hear their familiar honking. Yes, they're the snowbirds, hitting their horns as they speed through traffic to catch the flights that will take them to Phoenix for the next four months.

Some prefer Florida or California, but for Prairie types, perhaps partial to the dry air, Arizona is the preferred winter residence. In 1997 half of the 324,200 Canadians who visited the cactus state arrived between January and April. The majority were Canadian westerners. Their incentive is plain: they prefer sunburn to frostbite. Some are also motivated by health concerns: the dry air is great for arthritis or asthma. Once they arrive, they're usually welcomed by the year-round residents. Some American newspapers add a page of Canadian news, and local sports bars tune their satellite dishes to CFL games.

One particularly cold day, a friend of mine asked: "When is this global warming going to start?"

Three years of drought convinced farmers near Medicine Hat to invite Charles M. Hatfield, the self-promoting American rainmaker, to come and darken the skies with rain clouds. Hatfield arrived on April 20, 1921, and signed a contract with the town. He could claim credit for half the rain that fell within 160 kilometres of Medicine Hat from May 1 to August 1. He would be paid $2,000 per 2.5 centimetres, to a maximum of $8,000.

His method was suitably obscure to withstand any scientific queries that might have been made by the townsfolk: he erected a few towers in the country and placed chemical cocktails atop them.

Hatfield got results. The rain actually fell — just like it did in those regions that weren't paying for his services. Often it fell at the wrong time, and initially it lasted so long that it threatened seeding. Enough fell to secure the maximum payment for Hatfield, but after recurring complaints he settled for $5,500 from the United Agricultural Association. And he wisely got out of town.

Twister Tales

There's a reason why summer is tornado season. A twister occurs when hot air from the ground rises rapidly and collides with the cold air in the atmosphere. This mixing creates turbulent winds that spin upward. The revolutions pick up speed and create a column of air so powerful that it extends down to the ground as a funnel. Wind speeds can climb all the way up to 480 kilometres per hour inside the raging funnel. Twisters are awesome from far away, terrifying up close.

The Regina Cyclone of 1912 wasn't a cyclone at all. It was a tornado, and a bad one. In fact, it's still Canada's worst. It hit the city on June 30, a Sunday, and killed 28 people. The 365-metre funnel turned homes and businesses into kindling and left thousands of people homeless. Evidence of the twister's power was everywhere. Someone found a paper photograph embedded sideways in a wall! Damage reached $4 million — a lot of money back then. In fact, it was 47 years before all the rebuilding money loaned by the provincial government was repaid.

The black buzz saw that cut a pitiless path along the eastern edge of Edmonton on July 31, 1987, was a disaster movie come to screaming life. The mammoth funnel cloud narrowly missed some oil refineries before touching down on the Evergreen trailer park. Obviously loss of human life is the most relevant factor in judging a tornado's severity. The Edmonton tornado was nearly as deadly as the one that levelled Regina 65 years earlier. Twenty-seven people died, many of them denizens of the hapless trailer park. Across the city, 400 people lost their homes, but damage to commercial properties pushed the economic toll to $330 million.

Tornado Lite

The notion of watching a tornado may seem exciting, but it's mostly just terrifying. Thousands of Edmontonians can attest to that. A far less dangerous creature is the dust devil. It's a narrow column of spinning, heated air that stands about 200 metres tall. Dust devils can be seen on summer days dancing briefly across the prairie before disappearing.

The Truth Is Out Here

We have our superstitions. I encountered one while celebrating my first week of work at the *Medicine Hat News* in 1987. I joined some of my new co-workers at one of the Gas City's many bars, one of the few that didn't offer Live! Nude!! Girls!!! The waitress brought me a beer. I gave her a $2 bill. (Still around back then.) She looked at the wrinkled currency, raised an eyebrow, and said, "You must not be superstitious."

Some arcane local ritual about tipping? Nope. Two-dollar bills are bad luck on the Prairies. It goes back to their use at the turn of the century as the precise price for the services of a prostitute. Decades after inflation eroded that fee schedule, the deuce was still referred to as a "whorebill." (It's a moot point now. The paper bill has given way to the twoonie, which is only bad luck if you got stuck with one of the early defective mints with the removable centre.)

Somewhere in the mountains of Alberta lies the Lost Lemon Mine. Two prospectors named Lemon and Blackjack found a gold mine so rich that it drove the former to kill his partner. Afraid of the legal consequences, Lemon fled. He never found the mine again: nearby Natives had sealed it up to prevent a wave of prospectors. Legend has it that all who have tried to find it have met with accidents, violence, and death.

The Saulteaux First Nation believed that people could become possessed by the spirit of a *witigo* (a malignant, carnivorous Sasquatch, a second cousin to the werewolf). In 1906, in eastern Manitoba, one band decided to prevent future bloodshed by strangling a woman who had shown signs of possession. The police later heard of the ceremony, arrested several participants, and staged a jury trial. Modern law brushed aside Native beliefs and traditions, and the band's chief was convicted of murder and imprisoned for life.

Hundreds of years ago, before Europeans walked the Prairies, a meteorite fell to a spot not far from the Battle River, about 16 kilometres west of the Alberta-Saskatchewan border. Plains Indians called it the Manitou Stone, named after their creator. They saw in the iron stone the profile of a man's face and visited the spot as a place of worship. When a Methodist missionary named John McDougall dismissed the stone as a pagan symbol and removed it in 1866, misfortune quickly struck the Natives in the form of a disastrous winter, a miserable buffalo hunt, and a deadly smallpox epidemic. For them, this misfortune only confirmed the stone's power. The stone moved to several churches and museums across Canada before ending up in Edmonton's provincial museum in 1972. Curiously the legends surrounding the stone refer to an unusual characteristic. Reportedly no bigger than a man's fist when it first fell, the stone supposedly grew over time. It weighed about 90 kilograms when McDougall moved it and is now known to weigh 175 kilograms.

Edmonton toddler Erika Nordby survived a body temperature of 16°C after crawling outside one night in February, 2001.

There's an abundance of mythical beasts on the Prairies. Some exist in First Nations lore, and others crossed the Atlantic as mental luggage of the new Canadians.

- Manipogo has been spotted in Lake Manitoba, Dauphin Lake, and Lake Winnipegosis. The serpentine amphibian has been described as dark, slow-moving, and anywhere from nearly two metres long to several times that size. In the 1950s, the province's minister of industry and commerce even proposed a fact-finding expedition to solve the mystery.
- Cold Lake, straddling the border of Alberta and Saskatchewan, is rumoured to be home to a humpbacked white serpent named Kinosoo.
- The Sasquatch is most often associated with the forests of the Pacific Northwest, but Manitoba boasts more than 50 sightings of the tall, broad creature.
- Icelandic immigrants brought their story of the *mori*, the ghost of a young boy.
- St. François Xavier in Manitoba hosts a statue of a white horse that was ridden by a young Native man and his lover, who was promised to another man. When the pair were killed by their families, the horse escaped. Ever since, it has been seen running on the Plains.
- There have been tales, exchanged around the campfire, of a benevolent creature called "the Mid Winter." But no one's ever produced any evidence.

The Prairies are responsible for a disproportionate number of UFO sightings. Some eastern wag might interject at this point to explain that, no, those strange airborne machines are called "airplanes." (I envy those big-city types who can find the time to think of funny one-liners during the three hours that they spend in traffic each day.) In fact, the high number of sightings just makes sense, because our flat landscape must resemble one giant airstrip from space.

Explorers David Thompson and Andrew Davy reported Manitoba's first UFO sighting in the fall of 1792. While camping on Landing Lake, they saw a huge globular meteorite crash down on the ice fewer than 275 metres away. It made a noise "like a mass of jelly" (what on earth were they putting in jelly in those days?) and then shattered in an explosion of light. The next morning, they explored the apparent crash site and found no markings at all.

Modern-day Manitoba has contributed two great rashes of UFO sightings. The first occurred in the summer of 1952, when oddly moving lights of various colours and shapes started turning up in the sky. The activity peaked on August 13 when the lights appeared above Winnipeg in a series of formations over a three-hour period. From 1967 to 1969, Manitoba's skies once again seemed to be an arena for lights that hovered and dived. According to a few first-person accounts, some of the UFOs even touched down and opened their doors.

A Mystery of 360 Degrees

Crop circles have been found in fields around the world. Because they tend to occur in wheat fields, it's no surprise that the Prairies have hosted a few. The town that is perhaps best known for its circles is Langenberg, Saskatchewan, where several appeared in 1974.

 **The sand dunes near Lake Athabasca are as big as those in the Sahara — up to 30 metres high and 1.6 kilometres long. The sand dune field in northern Saskatchewan is about 300 square kilometres, the biggest in Canada.**

They are round, of course, up to 15 metres across, and give the appearance that something big and heavy has recently touched down, flattening the wheat. In more than a few cases here and abroad, they have proven to be the work of benign pranksters. Others are not so easily explained away. Some scientists have pinned the blame on spinning columns of ionized air.

Prairie Cures

I don't know if this cure worked, but it did make a dandy arts and crafts project. To cure the stomach flu, Natives tied two cups of dried flour in a cloth and boiled it for four hours. They let it cool and then scraped off the crust. The powdery scrapings were cooked in milk. Elders called it pap.

Low rainfall between Medicine Hat and Moose Jaw makes the region "the Dry Belt."

Plains Indians tackled the big health problems too. To treat tuberculosis, they laid a mustard poultice between two cuts of flannel. The pieces were quilted together, and this medicinal pillow was placed between the patient's shoulder blades. They may even have had a cure for the cold. They boiled the inner bark of a chokecherry bush and then strained and drank the resulting purplish red liquid.

First Nations and pioneers alike used wild roses to concoct a natural tonic for colds and rheumatism. They collected rosehips (the rose's spherical fruit), removed the stem and blossoms, and boiled them for 15 minutes in a little water. They then strained the mixture and sweetened one cup of the brew with four tablespoons of honey or sugar. One teaspoon of the tonic is reputed to contain as much vitamin C as at least one orange.

Prairie Architecture

The original Prairie building was, of course, the tipi. The frame was simply sturdy wooden poles lashed together at the apex. Tanned buffalo hides, sewn together with sinew, formed the cover. The bottom of the cover was anchored to the ground with heavy rocks. To this day, you can still find the discarded stones arranged in circles. Most tipis slept six to eight people and left room for their food, tools, and clothing. The tipi was the first mobile home. After it was disassembled, two of the wooden poles were lashed to a dog — and later to a horse — and became a carrying trailer dragged behind the animal. If you ever find a tipi circle while walking the prairie, look around. Appreciate the fact that, for a time, a family lived there.

The "Little House on the Prairie" really did exist. For the people who broke this land, it was home. It could have been a single room — the toilet was a cold winter's walk outside. Insulation didn't exist. Building supplies were in short supply: no trees meant no lumber. Besides, any wood was also needed for fuel, so the new settlers turned to the one resource that seemed endless: the land itself. The first homes were made of sod, the root-strewn clay found along creek beds. The sod was cut and shaped into cylinders and then stacked like bricks, grass side down. In its crudest form, the sod home was built into a hole dug into the side of a hill. Sod was built up around the front and sides for shelter and support.

When available, wooden poles were used to construct a tentlike frame for the roof. Hay and sod were laid overtop. It's a good thing that it rains so rarely on the Prairies, because the roof couldn't keep the rain out — it just delayed it. With its dirt floor, the sod house wasn't very clean. Still, it had its advantages. For one thing, it was warmer than a wooden home. A sod "building block" was more than half a metre long, 10 centimetres thick, and 30 centimetres wide! It also provided protection from fire, because sod doesn't burn. One other advantage: the sod hut cost nothing to build. Literally.

Lake Winnipeg is the sixth-largest lake in the country.

What is it about grain elevators? They've been called Prairie sentinels, which is as accurate as it is evocative. They stand guard over the communities beneath them, and, as long as they're there, it's a sign that things are still pretty good. When they disappear, it's a sign that the town is in trouble.

The elevator is really just a unique and impressive transfer point. It takes grain from the farmer's truck and "elevates" it so that it can be dropped into a storage area, where it remains until a train can take it away. That's why they're built along rail lines.

As soon as the first settlers had wheat to sell, moving it to the market was a challenge. The railway was clearly the best mode, but loading the railcars was a time-consuming, manual chore. It could take a farmer more than a week to load 650 bags of wheat into a single 1,300-bushel freight car. William Hespeler provided money to build the first grain elevator on the Prairies in 1878 at Niverville, Manitoba. It was round, squat, and, judging from the pictures, a little off-balance. Other businessmen built flat warehouses: some didn't even have roofs to protect the grain from precipitation and feathered moochers. In 1881 the first square-based elevator went up at Gretna, Manitoba, and a Prairie symbol was born.

68

Flour companies, local farm collectives, private firms such as the Pioneer Grain Company, and all three provincial wheat pools got into the elevator-construction business. By 1938 the skyline between Ontario and the Rockies had been altered by the presence of 5,758 elevators. Technology, coupled with the same forces that have been chipping away at rural life, has led to the abandonment of more and more of these unique structures. As the Prairies enter the new millennium, the number has fallen to less than 500.

One great elevator story. During World War II, British pilots learned to fly at air force training schools across the Prairies. One such pilot became lost during one exercise and radioed back for help. The advice tendered made perfect sense: find a rail line and follow it to a town. Each elevator sports the name of the town that hosts it, painted in big letters on its side. Thus, ground control advised the pilot to find the elevator, identify the town, consult a map, and head back to base. It didn't work. The pilot remained hopelessly lost. Exasperated, he radioed back that he had seen five different towns all called Pioneer, and none of them was on his map.

Only the barn can rival the elevator as a symbol of the Prairies. Variations in design and construction were linked to the ethnic origin of the farm family. Mennonite barns featured a row of windows above the entrance. Doukhobor barns were identifiable by the large overhanging roofs. With all varieties, form was subservient to function. These were essentially large sheltered spaces to accommodate animals, machinery, hay, and tools. The same quality — an abundance of space — made them natural buildings for social gatherings. The "barn dance" was a social hot spot until community halls came along in the 1940s and 1950s.

Winnipeg's most famous intersection is heralded as the coldest street corner in Canada. Portage and Main regularly reaches –40 degrees Celsius.

It took nearly two-thirds of a hectare of corrugated tin to cover the round roof atop what was surely the greatest barn the Prairies ever saw. The white barn — 120 metres long, 39 metres wide, and 18 metres high — was the crowning achievement of transplanted Kentuckian William "Horseshoe" Smith, a successful rancher and farmer in southwestern Saskatchewan. At its opening in 1914, the building was the site of a massive party — with a different orchestra performing at each end of the barn! It was a great conversation piece but not all that practical. Smith died in 1918, and three years later his pale monster was demolished.

The longest free-swinging, single-span footbridge in Canada sways over the Souris River in Souris, Manitoba. It was built in 1904 by a guy with a name right out of a Dickens novel — Squire Sowden. It was only a month old when a wind flipped it right over, necessitating the addition of supporting cables. Spring flooding tore the 177-metre structure from its moorings in 1976, but it's been rebuilt and still allows pedestrians a chance to feel like Indiana Jones.

The Cypress Hills of southwest Saskatchewan are the highest point between the Rockies and the Laurentians.

Built as a convent in 1846, St. Boniface Museum is the biggest oak-log building in North America.

The Vanishing Farm

For a time in the 1980s, that drought-ridden decade of farm bankruptcies and debt, people pondered the "death of the family farm." That was a bit premature. Agriculture is cyclical, like all industries. However, farms have grown larger and thus fewer in number. In Saskatchewan, for example, the number of farms fell by 11 percent between 1996 and 2001.

> "The way it's going, I would bet that there will only be half of us farmers left … Out here in this damn little town, when I was a kid, we had a dance every Saturday night and two picture shows a week. There was two poolrooms and two bowling alleys and two or three cafés in town. There was something to go to. Now the kids have to drive to Regina to get a bottle of beer or go to a show."
> — *Bert Wildfong, Craik, Saskatchewan*

A Good Place to Meet, Greet, or Eat

The residents of Balgonie, Saskatchewan, were reminded of how much the town rink means when they lost theirs.

70

When the kids in this bedroom community east of Regina played hockey, they had to avoid not only opponents' checks but also pieces of falling roof. So the community made a painful decision to tear down its aging facility and build a replacement. "It wasn't feasible to put any more money in and keep getting an engineer appraisal to open it up every year," says Kent Woods, a member of the local committee that oversaw the rebuilding campaign.

In 1996 a wrecker's ball completed the task that time had started, and Woods led a determined platoon of residents in a battle to raise $1.2 million. They raised $100,000 simply by knocking on 467 doors in Balgonie and another 250 homes in the surrounding area. They held bingos, approached corporate sponsors, and asked the town council to donate land and money. A sports auction and celebrity dinner brought in $25,000.

In the meantime, the hockey players and figure skaters drove to rinks in nearby communities. "Because the rink is such a focal point in the community, especially in the winter. That's all been taken out of Balgonie and spread out to other communities," Woods says. Even as formidable a force as small-town gossip has suffered. "You don't know the local news," Woods says. "There's not that communication link around town anymore."

The 3,000-year-old paintings and carvings that decorate the sandstone cliffs of Writing-on-Stone Provincial Park, south of Lethbridge, make up North America's largest rock-art collection.

Other benefits of a rink aren't so obvious. Woods quotes SaskSports figures claiming that crime falls by 16.3 percent in a community with a recreational facility. Towns that lose that facility typically see their crime rate jump by 11 percent.

"The rink is the central focal point of a community in small-town Saskatchewan ... You just go down there to hang out, just to see who's there, have a rink burger, whether you have anything to do or not."

Small-Town Life

"Some people don't like living in small communities because there's so many people know your business better than you do," Dick Heapy says. The farmer from Oak River, Manitoba, proves it too; over the course of the evening,

71

he and his drinking buddies at the local hotel exchange overt and veiled references to the fortunes and misfortunes of their neighbours, themselves, and the people who drift in and out of the bar. When people transgress the code of proper behaviour as it's understood in Oak River, they're never in the community doghouse for long. They all know each other too well for that. "There's always a bit of crap. Don't think there isn't, but small towns can be really forgiving," Dick says.

The five men sit around a long table next to the flashing, burping VLTs. The wives of four of them chat at the neighbouring table. A few other residents gamble away their loonies or sit at tables across the room. It's Friday night in Oak River. Older folks like Dick and his friends have a lot to talk about, and small-town people are champion talkers, drawing from their bank of shared memories. Younger people have less to talk about and even less to do. Earlier that evening, I watched three barely legal beer drinkers flip channels on the bar's big-screen TV, searching in vain for something worth watching. Eventually they left.

Oak River is comprised of 150 people, two unused grain elevators, one United Church, and some shops and homes spread out over half a dozen roads. Even in a cool autumn evening, the front door of every second home has been left wide open. "In the '50s and '60s, Oak River was the dance capital," Dick says. "We had orchestras in our rink." The Guess Who once played there. Even in the final year, the dance nights drew 400 people.

Tom Wilson was the first white to see Lake Louise and Emerald Lake.

Today it's a struggle. When one family moves on to make a better living somewhere else, that's one more family that won't be around to buy gas or eat at the cafés. Kids already go to nearby Rivers for high school, and it's unlikely that many of the 13 who just graduated will stick around. The doctor left, the men and women have to curl together in order to make up enough rinks, and the kids' hockey league includes teams from the two nearest towns. There used to be 13 grain elevators in the surrounding Rural Municipality of Blanshard, but they're all closed. The spur line through the area was shut down, taking a huge chunk of property taxes out of the RM's meagre coffers. It's worse down the road in Cardale, home to 19 people and two shops.

72

Towns like Oak River face the same economic forces as the family farm: "small" isn't deemed cost-effective. "It's very hard today to find a half-section farm," Dick says. "The margin of profit in grain farming today is so darn small that you need so many acres to do it." With smaller families, there's a smaller chance that one of the kids will want to take over the farm. So the parents sell the land to a farmer who can afford to expand. Farms grow in size and shrink in number. And the guy who sold? Well, he's no more likely to stick around than are the kids who graduate from the high school in Rivers. There's also an ongoing but small-scale reenactment of the immigration boom that first brought European farmers to the Prairies 100 years ago. Families from England, Sweden, Germany, and other European countries have been moving into the area, paying top dollar for large tracts of Blanshard's rich soil. Unfortunately that keeps land prices out of reach of Blanshard's own sons and daughters, even as it brightens the countryside with new faces and cultures.

Regina coughed through 19 dust storms in 1981 — a Canadian record.

"Farmers are asset-rich and cash-poor," Dick says. "You own the land, and you own the machinery, and that all has to be repaired and replaced, except that last time when you sell, and then you have a half-million dollars. The day before you sold it, you didn't have a half-million in the bank." His song is a familiar one, but he's also well aware of the job's rewards. "You're your own boss for 365 days a year. You have the opportunity to raise a family and grow up with nature. You see the seed planted, and you see the seed grow."

There have been some encouraging signs for Oak River. A big pipeline laid south of the town brought in workers to eat and sleep at the hotel. Some folks commute to new jobs at the massive hog plants that dot the region. The RM of Blanshard launched its own Web site and even used it to sell a house to a family from Halifax. And some optimist built a driving range on a field at the edge of town. Dick Heapy has a theory that a shrinking town will only decline so far. Then it's down to that core of people who are just too resilient to put down. That theory ties in to another of Dick's theories, the one about why small-town living is still the best. "Aw, hell, the people! The best people there is."

Chapter 4

Our Work Ethic

GEORGE HOFER: "YOU'VE GOT TO LOVE IT"

Like surprisingly graceful circus elephants moving through a choreographed dance number, four John Deere combines glide unerringly along predetermined patterns. They cost $250,000 apiece, and, as each follows a trail of freshly cut wheat, they repeatedly appear to be headed for a million-dollar collision. Instead, they pass within metres of each other and head off on their respective routes.

Sitting in his combine's air-conditioned cab, George Hofer steers the machine over the swaths of felled wheat, watching as it is churned headfirst by the combine's spinning auger into the inner recesses of the machine. The spinning drums inside the combine strip the kernels from each plant and drop them into the holding bin. The chaff is fired gracelessly out the back, producing

75

a curtain of dust that draws across the field. "You used to have to be out stooking this stuff," George says. A stook is a bundle of cut wheat, tied together in the shape of an hourglass. The image is featured on Saskatchewan's crest and flag. Like many Prairie symbols, it reflects what was rather than what is.

In his 30s, George has escaped that back-breaking era of farming, when the tractor's seat was hard metal and the hay bales were pitched by hand onto a hayrack. Grain farming isn't as physically hard as people think, George admits. But it is all-consuming during the three weeks of spring seeding and the six weeks of late-summer swathing and combining. At the moment, George is halfway through a workday that started at 7 a.m. and will finish around midnight. The long days in the field are mentally taxing, George says, but relaxing at the same time.

While farming has gotten easier, it's also grown more complicated. George runs the feed mill on the Arm River Hutterite colony, immediately north of the lovely Qu'Appelle Valley in south-central Saskatchewan. Year-round, his day starts at 7 a.m., but he's usually done mixing the feed for the colony's cattle, pigs, and chickens by suppertime. At night, he logs on to his computer. If necessary, he punches the keyboard to adjust the ingredients in the animals' feed. "Everything we do in our feedlot, I put it on the computer." Welcome to farming in the 21st century. You need to be an economist, a data specialist, and a geologist. And you should be prepared to pull a breech calf out of its mother.

Because they live communally and wear their culture in their everyday clothes, rather than as a costume reserved for annual festivals, Hutterites have gained an undeserved reputation as some closed, backward group, a sort of Canadian Amish. It's true that their religion — a strict, German Protestantism — doesn't allow them to watch television or listen to the radio.

But Hutterites are not Luddites, eschewing all the conveniences of the modern age. "Something new comes out, Hutterites are the first to own it," George says matter-of-factly. He describes the Green Star computer system installed in one of the colony's combines. The $15,000 program takes a satellite picture of a field and identifies where there's too little or too much protein or moisture and where there are weeds. Agriculture has undergone the same technological transformation as every other resource industry. That technology has enabled a farm to harvest 40 bushels an acre. But that technology costs money, George says. "Nowadays, inputs are so high you better have a 40-bushel wheat crop."

A Hutterite farm is a big farm — the Arm River spread is 6,500 hectares of wheat, canola, and barley, with large dairy and meat operations. Through decades of practice, Hutterites have refined bulk buying to an art. Like most farmers, each man has become an expert mechanic, welder, electrician, and handyman. But most farmers don't build a workshop the size of three barns, complete with its own coffeeshop and car wash. The investment in equipment goes well into the millions. There are 13 families at Arm River. If they were merely neighbours, each would require a combine. Because they live communally, they share labour and possessions and get the job done with the colony's five combines.

During roundup, the cowboy who minded the horses at night was the nighthawk.

"Farming, you have to be born to it," George says. "To go out late in life and become a farmer, forget it. You have to grow up on a farm." He wouldn't do anything else. "You think about it, you've got to leave something for the other guy. I want something for my kid when I'm not around anymore." Despite the changing tools of agriculture, this is something that hasn't changed: the notion of a relationship with the soil that can sustain one generation after another.

The Prairies were built by work. Indian tribes and homesteaders toiled in tough and sometimes dangerous conditions simply to feed themselves. Fur traders battled the elements and each other because their job required it of them. Work has also given the Prairies the very archetypes that identify us today: the farmer, the rancher, the oilman. It has determined not only how people live but also where they live. That's what happens in a resource-based economy. Prairie people have had a relationship with the land that's likely comparable to that between fishers and the sea. Throughout the 20th century, we have changed the ways in which we make a living from that land, diversifying into minerals, oil, lumber, and tourism and using technology to do it all more effectively than our ancestors did.

77

Putting It in Perspective

"Urban people think farmers are rich because they have land, equipment, and maybe even a four-wheel-drive tractor. But the farmer doesn't own the door handle on any of them."
— *Gordon Taylor, Landis, Saskatchewan*

 **Physicist Gerhard Herzberg left Nazi Germany and taught at the University of Saskatchewan from 1935 to 1945. He was a world authority on molecular structure, and in 1971 he won the Nobel Prize.**

For the agriculturally challenged (e.g., big-city CEOs, West Coasters, and every federal minister of agriculture), here's a quick introduction to our major Prairie crops:

- Red spring wheat: Saskatchewan grows it best, and we like to think that it makes the world's finest bread flour.
- Durum wheat: it produces high-energy bread and pasta.
- Rye: seeded in the fall, it produces rye bread, rye whisky, and cattle feed.
- Oats: the flour keeps fat from going rancid, so it's used in human foods such as peanut butter and in animal feed.
- Canola: the oil is used in margarine, salad dressing, and cooking oil, and the meal feeds animals.
- Barley: this drought-resistant plant is used in soups, flour, and beer but more often as livestock feed.
- Flax: Canada has been number 1 in global flax production since 1994; the oil is used in paint and flooring.
- Lentils: commercially grown in western Canada since 1972, lentils add protein to soups, stews, and vegetable dishes.
- Mustard: it is used in prepared mustard, of course, and spices, and the oil is used in emetics and other medicinal products.
- Peas: they are grown in the north because they require cooler temperatures and a lot of moisture.
- Canary seed: 85 percent of Canada's canary seed, a bird food, is grown in Saskatchewan.
- Sunflower: the oil is used in margarine and cooking oil, and the unshelled seeds are practically a Prairie hors d'oeuvre.

Combines Combined

What labour-saving devices do you employ in order to harvest 65 hectares in 15 minutes and 43 seconds? Get 64 friends. Sixty-five combines came together on a wheat field near Westlock, Alberta, on August 21, 1998. Before an audience of 3,000 people, the farmers worked together and set a world record for reaping the bounty from an entire quarter-section in the shortest period of time. The stunt was organized to raise a quarter-million dollars to build a water-diversion project in Ethiopia to facilitate — what else? — grain farming.

Maize Maze

"If you build it, they will come. And they will get lost." That's one possible motto for the latest variation on agriculture. Corn mazes have migrated from the United States to Manitoba, and customers are lining up to wander the rows cut into the 2.5-metre-high cornfields, seeking a way out. Mr. A Maze'n Corn, south of Winnipeg, is not as intricate as some of the elaborately sculpted and dramatically presented American corn mazes, but it is the longest, at 1.4 kilometres of trails. The maze opened August 8, 1998, and attracted 500 paying customers in its first five days. The puzzle can be solved, but the operators require all challengers to sign in and sign out, just in case someone gets lost. If that happens, don't worry. They'll stalk you.

A Woman's Touch around the Farm

Back in 1971, 95 percent of Canada's farms were exclusively run by men. By 2001 men ran only 64 percent of the nation's 276,550 farms, whereas women ran five percent. The rest were operated jointly by couples. The change reflects a greater role for women in the management of Canadian agriculture. Women are also, proportionately, more involved in specialty farms than men.

The biggest wheat field ever was seeded atop 14,175 hectares near Lethbridge in 1951.

"The first difficulty is not just dealing with one man, your husband, but with perhaps four men from your husband's family. You're dealing with egos, because when you start wanting to farm yourself you have to deal with men who don't want to be displaced by a woman."
— *Jeanne-Marie Crozier, farmer near Biggar, Saskatchewan*

A Very Full Day

As it was for the men, harvest was the busiest time of the year for the women. Here's a typical workday:

4:30 a.m.	milk the cows
5:30	make and serve breakfast for 20 or more men
7:00	wash the dishes
8:00	start baking, and then start making lunch for 20
noon	serve lunch
1:00 p.m.	wash the dishes, clean the house, care for the kids, get a start on supper
5:00	milk the cows again
6:30	serve supper
7:30	wash the dishes, clean, put the kids to bed, and prepare food for tomorrow.

A 1991 Stats Can survey found that female crop farmers had Canada's lowest-paid occupation at $12,421 per year.

In an Edmonton courtroom on July 1, 1916, Emily Murphy became the first female judge ever appointed in the British Empire.

Strength in Numbers

With the possible exception of a full CFL stadium, nothing on the Prairies illustrates our belief in collectivism like the farm cooperative. As the word implies, farmers get together, pooling resources from money and equipment to land and labour, to achieve what would be a harder and riskier proposition on their own.

There are all kinds of cooperatives across the Prairies; Saskatchewan's CCF government even formed a department to assist them in the 1940s. It was believed that the cooperative approach was an appropriate response to the rising costs of increasingly mechanized farming, the higher production demands during World War II, and the subsequent return of veterans seeking careers.

The farm cooperatives are formed between families or neighbours. All involve an appreciation of the pitfalls of cooperation, not simply the rewards.

There are meetings, disagreements, compromises, and more meetings. The farm co-op remains a rarity. In 1996 there were 746 active agricultural co-ops across the Prairies, but only 20 were farm co-ops. Some of the others dealt with agricultural supplies, livestock feedlots, and shared grazing land. And, of course, our farmers are joint owners of the provincial wheat pools that market their grain. For years, the biggest cooperative in the country, the Saskatchewan Wheat Pool, was also the nation's biggest handler of grain. However, the Alberta and Manitoba Wheat Pools — both co-ops — merged in 1998. The new company was called Agricore, and when it merged with United Grain Growers in 2002, the Saskatchewan Wheat Pool found itself in the unfamiliar position of being only the second-biggest grain handler in the country. When you add nonagricultural co-ops that meet needs such as housing and day care, the three Prairie provinces are home to roughly 2,500 cooperatives.

The name was Corne. The crop was not. Chevalier de la Corne planted the first wheat field in western Canada in the Carrot River valley in what is now Saskatchewan, way back in 1754.

Cowboys

Canadian ranching started in central British Columbia and spread to the drier, southern grasslands of Alberta and southwestern Saskatchewan. The first ranchers tended to be retired Mounties who enjoyed horsemanship and the outdoors or British gentlemen who came over with enough money to finance a new ranch. The first ranchers enjoyed relative freedom to pursue their tough but lucrative livelihood (all the more profitable once the CPR provided them with easy transport). It was the rush of homesteaders around the turn of the century that saw farming overtake ranching across much of the Prairies.

The roundup is ranching's equivalent of the harvest. The cattle that roam free over the open pastures each summer have to be gathered up in the fall and brought back to the ranch, where they can be fed and kept over winter. Cowboys from the different ranches worked in teams, heading out across the open range. They drove the cattle into a large central herd. The cattle were then separated according to their brands and taken to their ranch's designated range.

Members of the Savill family didn't saddle up when it was time to round up their livestock. They put on bike helmets. Since 1991 the Savills have used mountain bikes to herd the 100 cattle at their ranch near Balzac, north of Calgary. As Trish Savill pointed out, you don't have to feed a bike, and you can't throw a horse over a fence.

 **The Royal Canadian Mint in Winnipeg makes all Canadian coins and produces coins for more than a dozen other countries — or about three billion coins a year.**

Cowgirls

A $10 fine was levied against the young Cardston woman who reacted in 1900 to an insulting comment in a way that was very Wild West if not exactly lady-like. The rancher's daughter went and got her gun (was her name Annie?). She found her critic and forced him at gunpoint to kneel and apologize.

Lady Ernestine Hunt was doubly rare: a rancher, and a cowgirl. The globe-trotting daughter of the Marquis of Allesbury was not yet 30 when, in 1906, she moved to western Canada to go into the cattle business. She leased 16,200 hectares southwest of Calgary.

Rural Medicine

Dr. Wilfred Bigelow learned a lesson in homestead medicine when he travelled out from Brandon one January night in 1908 and headed for a distant farm-house to help an expectant mother. When Bigelow arrived, he encountered not only the young mother but also an elderly midwife, sitting in a chair and calmly smoking a clay pipe. The older woman advised him that the patient's labour pains had started the day before but showed no signs of speeding toward the desired conclusion. "I think we will have to quill her," the midwife suggested. Bigelow didn't know what she was talking about, but he didn't want to appear uninformed. Pretending that he knew what she meant, he replied: "I hope we can get along without quilling."

The young doctor examined his patient, administered some medication, and waited. Nothing happened. The midwife suggested quilling several times, until the doctor, by then curious, decided that it was worth a shot, whatever it was. "You go ahead and do it," he suggested.

The woman walked over to a goose wing hanging from a nail above the stove. She extracted a long quill, cleaned it, cut off both ends, and dipped one end into a package of cayenne pepper. Bigelow followed the midwife into the patient's bedroom and watched as she inserted the quill into the younger woman's nostril. She blew the pepper up into the patient's nasal cavity. "Doc," the elderly woman advised, "you'd better get ready." The pregnant woman immediately started sneezing. Within minutes, Bigelow was holding the long-awaited newborn.

When it came to their teeth, many people who weren't flush with money preferred to let their dental health slide. Dr. Paul Bookhalter recognized that many rural folk couldn't afford to drive in to Regina for treatment, so in the 1950s he started "barnstorming." One day each week, the young dentist would wake up at 4 a.m., rent a car for the day, and drive to a small town within a 160-kilometre radius of Regina. He set up his office wherever he could and charged $1 for an extraction and $2 for a filling. The approach sometimes demanded compromises. In Imperial, he couldn't fit his portable dentist's chair into the doctor's office that he used. "So I used to sit the patient on the toilet," he says from his home in Regina. In Stoughton, he worked inside the fire hall, setting up his chair between the jail cell and the parked fire truck. "I laid my instruments out across the truck's big fender." One morning, the fire hall wasn't available, so Bookhalter relocated to a seldom-used community hall in the middle of a field. He remembers working over one patient and feeling a cool breath against the back of his neck. "A horse had walked across the field and into my office."

Unwanted seeds that spring up in a field are called volunteer grain.

Black Gold

There are two dates that stand out in the history of Alberta. The first is February 13, 1947. That was the day an Imperial Oil crew struck oil northeast of Leduc after weeks of drilling. Alberta would never be the same: the high-quality crude tapped on that day would fuel automobiles and the provincial economy for years to come. The well pumped crude until 1974.

The second date? August 9, 1988: the day that Wayne Gretzky was traded to the L.A. Kings. His departure was the beginning of the end for the Edmonton Oilers: their well went dry too.

Wildcatting is synonymous with risk-taking. It's a roll of the dice, and a virgin field is the crap table. A wildcat well is one drilled in a region where oil has not been discovered. Many wildcats come up dry, but one strike will lead to more as the new oil field's wealth is exploited.

Edmonton's role as gateway to the North was cemented when construction started on the Alaska Highway in 1941.

Alberta's oilmen met their fiery match in Canadian Atlantic Well no. 3 in the Leduc oil fields. The well was a problem almost as soon as it was drilled. For months, it lost $50,000 worth of oil and natural gas each day, leaking it out everywhere except the wellhead. Crews pumped 91 tonnes of mud, water, cement, sawdust, and even golf balls into the drillhole to plug the well's bleeding arteries. In early September 1948, the inevitable happened. The well ignited, creating sky-high flames over a 16-hectare oil field. It took firefighters several days to flood the well with enough water to quell the fire and end no. 3's short, tumultuous life.

Boom!

When the oil industry in Alberta took off like a rocket, the two major cities divided the rewards between them. Due to its proximity to the fields, Edmonton got the well-paid rig workers, whereas Calgary got the head offices and all those gleaming skyscrapers to house them. The men who worked the oil patch and took home those big cheques spread that good fortune around. Edmonton saw a lot of money change hands in the 1970s. Trickle-down economics actually worked, because nearly everybody had money.

And Bust

All good things come to an end. So did the oil boom. In 1986 the glut of world oil supplies drove the price down from $30 per barrel to less than $10. More than a few long sedans with worn tires and fading paint sported a bumper sticker that read "Oh, please Lord, give me another boom, and I promise not to piss this one away."

And Boom Again!

The oil and gas roller coaster rides on, but Alberta is handling the ups-and-downs a lot better than it used to. Throughout the late 1990s, oil was still under-performing, but by that time the provincial economy wasn't balanced on a single pillar. Food processing, pulp and paper, chemicals and natural gas had all grown to form bigger slices of the province's economic pie. By the summer of 2003, oil was back over $30 per barrel; oil and gas now account for 23 percent of Alberta's GDP. And those other industries have grown in step. Food-processing revenues were $3.5 billion in 1983. By 2002, the figure had reached $9.8 billion. And, of course, Canadians seeking jobs continue to march into Alberta.

A similar story is occurring in Saskatchewan. Its heartbeat nearly flatlined in the 1980s when farm debt and an overreliance on wheat made it very much a have-not province. Again, diversification on the farm and beyond, notably in the potash industry, has sparked renewal.

Here's how you "stook." Gather six bundles of ripe grain. Sit two upright in the middle, with two on each side to prevent the wind from blowing the bundles over. That's a stook.

The biggest benefactor of the boom is Calgary. Only Toronto has more head offices in Canada. Calgary's ascendance was epitomized by Canadian Pacific's decision to relocate there from Montreal in 1996.

In a newspaper article, University of Calgary economist Frank Atkins described the reaction on Bay Street: "The east up until recently looked at us as Cowtown. We were a bunch of hicks riding around in pickups with white cowboy hats. We kept trying to tell them a lot of head offices were moving here, but they buried their heads until Canadian Pacific moved here."

Manitoba's geography has permitted diversification of another kind. Private hydroelectric power companies such as Winnipeg Electric and the Brandon Electric Light Company started building the industry back in the 1880s. The provincial government shut down the private companies in 1933 and created the Manitoba Power Commission. Three years later, MPC sold power to out-of-province buyers (Minnesota and North Dakota) for the first time.

Today sales to its Canadian and American neighbours account for a big chunk of Manitoba Hydro's profits.

From 1996 to 2001, 37,600 people left Saskatchewan for Alberta's bright lights. B.C. saw even more people migrate to Alberta: 89,700.

ENTREPRENEURS: CAN'T SPELL "RICHARDSON" WITHOUT "RICH" OR "SON"

The Richardsons are synonymous with the kind of business success that has withstood the twin tests of time and the bottom line. The financial and agricultural megacorporation has been a family-run business since its modest beginnings in 1837. The sparkplug came in the form of James "Jim" Armstrong Richardson, who joined the family company in 1909. At the time, James Richardson and Sons was simply a grain exporter. Jim became president in 1919, the year that he moved from Ontario to the Winnipeg office. From that point on, his business was as much building the west as profiting from it. He started Richardson Securities in 1925 and built it into one of Canada's biggest investment houses (later Richardson Greenshields Securities, which was taken over by RBC Dominion Securities in 1996). In rapid succession, Jim invested in a range of new industries, forming Western Canada Airways and then a radio station. The family business grew to include Richardson Real Estate; Pioneer Shipping; Pioneer Grain, Feed, and Fertilizer; Richardson Terminals; and Richardson Stock Farms.

Prolonged exposure to soil and grain dust creates a condition called farmer's lung.

Jim Richardson Jr. took the helm of the company in the 1960s before being elected as the Liberal MP for Winnipeg South and eventually serving as Pierre Trudeau's minister of both defence and supply and services.

It makes sense that Manitoba's greatest success story should be marked by an equally impressive building. The stock market crash of 1929 postponed construction of the Richardson Building, but the version finally built in the 1960s became, at 32 storeys, Winnipeg's tallest building.

The West Edmonton Sprawl

When Edmontonians visit, they talk about the mall. As in "You've got to come and see the mall. They've got shark tanks now!" This enthusiasm is understandable. When you live in a world that has made a religion out of consumerism, you're going to brag about living near the Vatican.

Marquis wheat is pronounced mar-kwis, not mar-kee.

Yet, when out-of-towners finally visit their friends in Edmonton, they often encounter a very different attitude. "You go without me," the host is likely to say. "I can't stand going near the place." This reluctance is also understandable. It's easy to get tired of a place that is so crowded, so busy, and so big. Brothers Eskandar, Raphael, Nader, and Bahman Ghermezian opened the West Edmonton Mall in 1981. It expanded in 1983 and in 1985 and will usher in the new millennium with "phase 4." At 5.3 million square metres, it is the largest mall in the world.

What started out as a showy display of shopping opportunities and family recreation mutated. There's a rink with public skating (except when the Oilers hold one of their periodic practices there). You can ride the same roller coaster that malfunctioned in 1987 and killed two people. It's safer now; like most everything else at the 44.5-hectare mall, it's either improved or expanded. There's even a beach with a machine-generated surf. Is this a mall or a biosphere? There's a casino, a bowling alley, a theatre complex, and a hotel with theme rooms. And there are more than 800 stores, so, yes, you can even shop.

Successful entrepreneurship doesn't have to involve industry, mergers, and stock dividends. In the case of onetime Winnipeg resident J. W. Conklin (1892-1970), it had more to do with cotton candy, bumper cars, and three balls for a quarter.

Brooklyn-born "Patty" Conklin founded his midway concession in 1929. Conklin Shows became the largest travelling midway in the world. In 1937 Conklin provided the midway at the Canadian National Exhibition and opened the world's first Kiddieland. If you've been to a summer fair, you have Patty to thank for the wild rides and the nausea.

Harry Wasylyk used polyethylene, one of the new materials that emerged after World War II, to design the first plastic garbage bag in his Winnipeg kitchen. His story reveals how one good idea can lead to another. Wasylyk began selling polyethylene gloves to the Winnipeg General Hospital. That's how he learned that the hospital had trouble keeping its garbage cans sanitary. He created the plastic garbage bag to be placed inside the cans.

When Union Carbide bought Wasylyk's business, it tried to expand the market for the bags, with little initial success. Many municipalities decided that it was illegal to leave garbage out on the curb for pickup if it was in bags rather than in the traditional metal cans. In 1969 Union Carbide expanded its line of Glad plastic products (formerly restricted to sandwich bags and plastic wrap) by introducing Glad garbage bags. Promoted by the familiar snow-peaked Man from Glad, Wasylyk's invention finally caught on.

Some people wrestle with moral issues, analyzing them, debating them, and ultimately abiding by them. Winnipeg writer Henry Makow turned them into a board game. Featuring cards with all sorts of ethical dilemmas, *Scruples* has sold millions of copies since it was introduced in 1985.

 **Great West Life's new head office in Winnipeg in 1958 opened the door to a new way of doing business: it housed the first computer in western Canada.**

Not all Prairie businesspeople have been successful. Sir George Simpson, the governor of the Hudson's Bay Company and for a time the patriarch of the Red River Settlement, devised several luckless business ventures for those early settlers. He promoted the Buffalo Wool Company, badly run and unable to generate much interest in buffalo wool. Its failure cost the HBC $25,000. Simpson later concluded that perhaps sheep were better for wool production and sent a team of horsemen to Kentucky to get some. They left the state with 1,500. By the time they reached the settlement, only 251 were left. The short-lived Flax and Hemp Company suffered from one flaw: there was absolutely no market for either product.

Here's a curious fact: the first commercial existed long before the first television show. Manitoba farmer James Freer made a film about life on the prairie in 1897. The following year, it was shown in the United Kingdom to sell Canada to potential emigrants. Millions of people later, we can assume that this ploy worked.

The three Prairie provinces grow all but 10 percent of Canada's barley and rye.

He Dared to Dream Big

Tom Sukanen could build anything, except a boat ride back home. Still, it's amazing how close he came.

In 1911 the Finland-born Sukanen left his family in Minnesota to become a homesteader in Saskatchewan. Over the years, the mechanically inclined Sukanen built pretty much anything he needed: a thresher, a violin, a bicycle, a working car. When he tired of farming, he decided to build a 13-metre ship, one that he could pilot all the way back to Finland. He mapped out a route along the South Saskatchewan River into the Atlantic Ocean.

Using scrap metal, Sukanen completed the steamship's three sections: keel, hull, and cabin. He painstakingly hauled the sections to the river's edge 27 kilometres away, where he intended to assemble them. He never did. Sukanen was committed to North Battleford's mental hospital and died soon after in 1943. Some parts of the failed project were later salvaged and moved to a museum 14 kilometres south of Moose Jaw in recognition of Sukanen's unfinished business.

Winnipeg-born Sir William Stephenson won medals for bravery as a World War I pilot, invented the wireless photo-transmission process while a student at the University of Manitoba, and became Winston Churchill's top espionage agent in North America during World War II. In 1945 he was knighted. Called "the Quiet Canadian," he is better known as Intrepid, Canada's most famous spy.

A key phrase from the counterculture lexicon was created in Saskatchewan. Working principally in Weyburn, two doctors conducted experiments with mescaline and other hallucinogens and combined the Greek words for "mind" and "expanding" and came up with *psychedelic*. One of the doctors, Humphry Osmond, later travelled to Hollywood and provided mescaline to Aldous Huxley. The American author incorporated the experiences into his writing.

They Built a Better Mousetrap

- That James Gosling was blessed with both technical deftness and rogue creativity was evident when he was just 12: the farmboy from outside Calgary played Frankenstein with a telephone switch and an old TV set to create an electronic version of tic-tac-toe. Nearly 30 years later, the University of Calgary graduate invented Java, the universal language for computerized products used around the world.

- The echoes of John Hopps's work have been beating for years, and with each beat someone, somewhere, gets another moment of life. The Winnipeg native earned a degree in electrical engineering from the University of Manitoba before joining the National Research Council in Ottawa. In the 1950s, Hopps built the first pacemaker to electrically stimulate the beating of the human heart. In 1985 he got one himself.

- The Bechard brothers of Lajord, Saskatchewan, bestowed a mighty change on farming by inventing the air seeder. It's a pricey piece of equipment but a vast improvement over the old manual technique and a boon to modern farmers.

- Charles N. Pogue may have been a great inventor — we'll never know. In 1938 the Winnipeg man claimed that he had invented a new vehicle carburetor that got 322 kilometres to the gallon. The Pogue carburetor used a long spiral bottle to heat and vaporize the fuel before it entered the engine cylinders — 10 times more effectively than a standard carburetor. One Winnipeg-to-Vancouver trial run achieved 209.3 kilometres to the gallon. Unfortunately Pogue announced a few months later that someone had entered his workshop and stolen his working models. Maybe, but one theory holds that an oil company simply made him an offer that he couldn't refuse.

Manitoba has more than 21,000 farms.

Prairie Nobel-ity

As of 2003, 17 Canadians had won Nobel Prizes, perhaps the most prestigious award in the world. Three came out of the Prairies.

Henry Taube had been an American citizen for 42 years when he won the Nobel Prize for chemistry in 1983. However, this Stanford University chemistry professor was born in Neudorf, Saskatchewan, and attended the University of Saskatchewan. Taube won the prize for his work on "the mechanism of electron transfer reactions, particularly of metal complexes." No surprise there. I wish I had a nickel for every time I heard that old topic bandied about the coffeeshop.

Colin Low, from Cardston, Alberta, co-directed *Labyrinth* in 1967, the precursor to the big-screen IMAX format.

Lethbridge-born Bertram Brockhouse was a co-winner of the 1994 prize for physics for his work on neutron spectroscopy. Simply put, it enables us to study the activity of a substance's atoms by beaming neutrons through it. (Well, those of us with a neutron spectroscope lying around the house.) That's a long journey from his days on a farm in the Milk River district.

Richard Taylor actually won two Nobel Prizes by thinking small. The native of Medicine Hat was part of a team that won the Nobel Prize for physics in 1979 for its work in the field of subatomic particles. In 1990 he and his two American co-researchers, Jerome Friedman and Henry Kendall, won the same award for discovering the smallest thing in the universe. (No, it wasn't Ralph Klein's social conscience.) Taylor, who had moved to Stanford in 1952, and his two peers showed that protons and neutrons are made up of even smaller natural particles called quarks. They used Stanford's linear accelerator to bang subatomic particles together at high speeds. Think of very small, very fast bumper cars.

What is it about Prairie brains and Stanford?

First, Biggest, Greatest

One of the things that defines us is an unabashed pride in accomplishments that would be overlooked in larger cities. To recognize the invention of the Symons oilcan right in its own backyard, the town of Rocanville, Saskatchewan, built an 8.5-metre-high version. It's the world's largest oilcan, although there's probably not much competition. Here are some other achievements:

- Reaching speeds of 96 kilometres per hour, the pronghorn antelope of southern Alberta and Saskatchewan is Canada's fastest mammal.

- The world's longest, highest trestle bridge is the CPR High Level Bridge spanning the Oldman River valley in Lethbridge.
- The world's biggest tomahawk stands 16.5 metres high and weighs more than 5,225 kilograms. So why is the Saskatchewan town that hosts it called Cut *Knife*?
- A statue of the world's largest mosquito exists at Komarno, Manitoba. Why any community would want to honour one of the banes of the Prairies beats me. Was the wind chill cenotaph already spoken for?
- What's aluminum, seven metres tall, 5.5 metres wide, and has more patterns than a Hutterite fashion show? The world's largest pysanka. The huge painted Easter egg sits at the eastern edge of Vegreville, Alberta.
- The mascot of Porcupine Plain, Saskatchewan, is Quilly Willy, whose statue is billed as the largest of its kind in the world. Believe it or not, it's a porcupine.
- Canada's best glass of water reportedly pours from a spring in Nanton, Alberta.
- Edouard Beaupré was known as the Willow Bunch Giant because he stood eight foot three and weighed just under 400 pounds. His feet reportedly dragged on the ground when he rode a horse, further ruining any hope that he might have had for a career as a jockey.

Chapter 5

Our Wonderful Food

ROLANDE RHEAULT: MATRON OF THE FALL SUPPER

Six hours of work and 400 degrees of cooking power have put a healthy sheen on Rolande Rheault's upper lip, forehead, and cheeks. They have also made her tired, but her work is almost finished. The 18 turkeys and 50 bags of once-frozen vegetables are spending their final minutes in the huge baker's oven, and 174 kilograms of potatoes have been boiled, mashed, and packed into metal trays. "This morning the men came and carved all the turkeys. My daughter cooked them last night," Rheault says, her francophone accent and cheery manner bending her words into pleasing shapes and sounds.

Rheault studies the stacked insulated containers of food as they're carted out the door into waiting trucks. "Oh, God, talk about potatoes, eh?" She and another woman wipe down the large counter. Behind them, another woman shouts: "What do you want, Ken?" He answers in French, the occasional English word slipping through. The half-dozen people in the large kitchen don't slow down, even though their chores for the St. Anne fall supper are finally at an end.

Prairie fall suppers are decades old, and they prove that eating is as much about who's next to you as what's in front of you. In St. Anne, the fall supper is the biggest social event of the year. It has a long history in this francophone town outside Winnipeg, even though it disappeared for much of the 1980s due to lack of interest. The town revived the practice in 1991, and the residents welcomed it back: 800 people sat down to the meal in 1997. The fall suppers turned out to be good practice for St. Anne's cooks. During the Red River flood of 1997, when parts of southern Manitoba turned into swampland, 400 residents of the nearby Roseau River Indian Reserve were cut off from their homes by the rising waters. For four weeks, they slept on cots in St. Anne's rink and ate meals prepared by the women of the town.

Rheault debates whether or not to go home, clean up, and attend the supper. She would like to take a nap, she confides. "You're not even hungry. You see it all day."

French is the mother tongue for the vast majority of St. Anne's 1,600 residents, so perhaps it's a little disappointing that the menu doesn't reflect that background. Tourtière, the French meat pie, is easy to find at Christmas dinners, but it's absent from the fall supper. The reduced variety is due in part to the fact that the food is now prepared at one location. Before the catering kitchen and its immense seven-rack oven were available, each fall supper was cooked in several hundred ovens around St. Anne, and the result was a wider array of dishes. For the desserts, anyway, that's still the procedure. "We'll have pies for dessert," Rheault promises. "That's all given away by the ladies of the town. There will be all kinds of pies."

During the Depression, a beverage was made from dried and ground dandelion roots.

She doesn't lie. When the doors to the Legion hall open at 4 p.m., the first diners encounter two long rows of salads, veggies, potatoes, meatballs, and turkey before arriving at two tables completely covered with pies. There are

180 different pies: blueberry, cherry, apple, pecan, and pumpkin, each bearing its maker's preference for either a solid pastry top or the old-fashioned cross-hatched style. Those not eaten will be sold, and the proceeds, like the money from the $8 supper tickets, will go toward repairs to St. Anne's pretty century-old church.

But the good cause has to be coupled with good food. "If you go to a fall supper and the food is not good, you don't go back the next year," says Mary Perron, who leaves the cooking to Madame Rheault's crew but oversees all other aspects of the supper herself. She is barely able to take two bites from her own plate without one of the many volunteers asking her for something.

The supper runs until 7 p.m., and the lineup to get in never falters until at least 6:30. Many of the people are former residents who time their return visits to coincide with the supper. All around, people are catching up, and the cacophony rises and falls in waves. Some, curiously, eat in silence. The emcee periodically warns people that there are only a few minutes left to buy tickets for the door prizes. One of the prizes is a live pig. Unlike the socket set and the knitted afghan, it is not on display. One mother laughingly tells her friends that her son deposited all their tickets in the draw bag for the pig. "He better not win."

Not everyone drinks. Some people don't dance. But everybody eats. So an event at which people raise money by eating a meal much like those at home becomes a rare chance for half the residents of a community to simply sit down together. I never do see Madame Rheault in the hall. I guess she took that nap.

Most of the people who saw the 1996 film *Fargo* laughed at the painfully earnest and perpetually awkward characters, but we, in typical Prairie fashion, laughed *with* them. We were, in effect, laughing at ourselves. The twisted crime caper is set in North Dakota, but it contains numerous references that Canadian flatlanders recognize. The film was a cult hit, especially gratifying because most of the time the only thing considered "cutting edge" about Prairie life is the swather.

Of all *Fargo*'s keen observations, none provoked a bigger laugh than the simple shot of two characters parading down a buffet line, filling their plates with one artery-clogging food after another. This is one truism of Prairie food. Starch rules. Potatoes, pasta salad, perogies, even dinner buns. They are the fuel that protects us from the harsh winter climate. Whoever wrote that scene has been to a few Sunday brunches.

So here's to *Fargo*. However, just to set your mind at ease, I should point out that we saw absolutely nothing familiar in the scene in which one person stuffs another into a tree shredder.

Food of the First People

For centuries, buffalo were at the centre of the Plains Indian way of life. A walking Wal-Mart, a bison provided the Narives with an array of necessities. Foremost, it was a source of meat. The tongue and organs were delicacies. Beyond those, here's what one bison could provide:

fragments of shoulder blade = paint applicators

grease = mixed with ochre to make paint

tail = used to sprinkle hot water on rocks inside the sweat lodge

skull = used in the Sun Dance ceremony

horn = a cup or a canteen for carrying food on journeys

sinew = thread for sewing

the hide = clothing, blankets

rawhide = an excellent fastener, because it could be tied wet and would tighten as it dried

bladder bag = a container for fat

dung = fuel

One kilogram of flour makes two loaves of bread.

There really were dishes such as boiled reindeer head, bear-fat pastry, moose in a blanket, and pickled beaver tail. All of them were pretty much what their names imply. Likely no race has ever eaten more meat than pre-contact Plains Indians; they needed protein for their physically challenging existence.

Métis dishes are blends of the ingredients and preparation practices of the First Nations and French cultures. They include versions of the above dishes as well as those that reflect a French background, including tourtière — a pie of ground pork and beef usually served at the Christmas Eve meal — and *les boulettes* (meatballs).

The beef jerky sold in cellophane packets in convenience stores everywhere first came into being among the First Nations tribes of the Canadian west. They cut bison meat into thin, flat strips and stretched them out along racks made from willow branches. The meat was left to dry in the sun for up to four days. Later, pioneers adopted that method of preserving meat. They added salt for flavour. Somewhere along the line, somebody called it jerky.

In 1994 Brian Petracek became the first Saskatchewan farmer to harvest a field of dill seed at his farm near Gerald.

Pemmican was simply buffalo meat dried, cooked briefly, and then laid out flat and beaten to a powder. The meat was dumped into a buffalo-hide bag and mixed with buffalo fat and flavourful ingredients such as dried saskatoon berries or chokecherries. In this form, it kept well and became a staple of the winter diet for fur traders and other early inhabitants.

Bannock. It sounds like a cop show from the 1970s. In fact, it's a real Prairie staple — and so integral to our culinary heritage that we named a town after it (a sawmill community in northeastern Saskatchewan). The name is Scottish, given by the early fur traders. Made from flour, salt, soda, melted fat, and water or milk, bannock was kneaded into a thick, round pancake and fried in a pan. Traders and early settlers ate it so often that surely they would have died without it.

Typical of their efficient approach to getting the most out of their game animals, the Plains Cree singed moose nose over an open flame, then scraped and washed it before boiling it. They considered it a delicacy. And I'm just going to take their word for it.

Storing, Freezing, Cooking, Canning

With no refrigeration, settlers stored vegetables in a root cellar or a root house. The latter place was preferable because it was cooler and less messy, and any odours didn't waft up into the home. Sometimes the simple wooden structure was built into the side of a hill, with soil packed around the cracks and seams. A vertical pipe out the top ensured ventilation but necessitated the small chore of clearing snow from it during the winter.

Beans also stored well, and they were cheap and easy to prepare. One frontier Mountie assigned to a remote post relied on the bean's simplicity and

97

hardiness to feed himself throughout the winter. Like a squirrel storing nuts, he packed an enormous amount of baked beans into women's stockings and nailed these unusual containers to the exterior of his home (a panty pantry?). Throughout the winter, he chopped off as much of the frozen legume as he needed for each meal and heated it up.

The rear gate on a chuckwagon folded down, providing the cook with a working space. The chuckwagon was a kitchen on wheels during cattle drives, and a skilled cook was greatly appreciated. (Was this where tailgate parties came from?) A wagon typically carried enough food to feed up to 20 men for several weeks. Because of the weight that it had to carry — food, pots, water, a stove — the chuckwagon was sturdier than your average covered wagon.

It was some years before western settlers could afford or even obtain proper kitchen stoves, so they "made do." These cooking and heating devices reflected the lack of available resources as well as the ethnic backgrounds of their owners.

Métis settlers built mud stoves. They were basically indoor fireplaces, built with a mixture of hay and mud and finished with clay. Cooking pots were hung from iron bars positioned above the stove.

The Ukrainian bake oven travelled from eastern Europe to Canada. It consisted of a square log base reinforced with stone. Its overhead cooking chamber was made by binding willow branches together in a curved shape (a bit like a lobster trap). The frame was coated with plaster made from clay, sand, and horse manure. (It's possible that, without the horse, nothing much would have been built on the Prairies.) This oven — which existed with minor variations among other ethnic groups — cooked food by retaining heat from the coals burned inside and then raked out before cooking began.

Some Fuel-Proof Substitutes

Settlers on the flat landscape usually had to travel long distances several times a year to obtain wood for cooking and heating. This supply wasn't always sufficient, so they turned to dried buffalo chips. Accessible trees, like the buffalo, eventually disappeared. Settlers turned to anthracite coal, but it was expensive. The lignite coal found in southern Saskatchewan was cheaper but didn't burn nearly as effectively. Some families used straw or hay if their livestock could spare it.

A lot of Prairie recipes end with the words "pack into sterilized jars and seal." Around here, vinegar is an essential ingredient, and sealing jars are a kitchen necessity. We're crazy about canning and proud of our preserves. The habit began in country kitchens, long before refrigeration, and remains a popular way to "put up" jams, vegetables, and fruits for the winter.

> "Wouldn't that jar your grandmother's preserves?"
> — *rural Manitoba expression*

Always the culinary pioneer, Saskatoon was home to Canada's first Kentucky Fried Chicken outlet in 1958.

Food from the Old Country

Polish sausage, Russian borscht, Icelandic vinarterta: they reflect the true nature of Prairie food, which is as varied as that on the tables of Europe. The one constant is that it is very much "home cooking" and is more likely to turn up at a picnic than on a restaurant menu.

Of all these dishes, the perogie reigns supreme. I'm sure that somewhere on the Plains there's a giant statue of one. This soft, boiled purse of dough stuffed with a variety of fillings is the starch of choice in a region that can't get enough carbohydrates. Perogie dough is made from flour, eggs, and sour cream. The soft dough is cut into circles, filled with stuffing, and pinched closed. Dump the perogie (*pyrohy* or *varenyky* in Ukrainian) in boiling water; when it's ready, it will rise to the surface. A perogie can be eaten as is, deep-fried, or fried in a pan. Although it sounds way too simple to be a delicacy, a perogie swimming in butter and crowned with a dollop of sour cream is, for my money, the quintessential Prairie taste — succulent yet *hearty*. I prefer 'em without fried onions, though many folks consider that a necessary finishing touch.

One of the most treasured recipes that Icelandic families brought to Gimli and points west was vinarterta. Christmas cake. The cake mix is pretty straightforward, but it's as much a work of structural design as culinary craft. Eight round cakes, each measuring 20 centimetres across, are stacked on top of each other, separated by a sweetened prune filling. Store the upright pastry in a container for several days before topping it with butter icing and serving.

99

A Prairie town might not have a hospital, a grain elevator, or even a school, but it almost certainly has a restaurant with a sign that reads "Chinese-Canadian Cuisine." Hundreds of these family-run eateries have dotted the Prairies for decades.

Nature's Gifts

The saskatoon berry is held in near reverence around here. It looks like a blueberry, but it's more of a purple colour and has a nutty centre. The pearl-sized berry grows on the prairie shad bush and added flavour to pemmican. The word *saskatoon* is Cree for "fruit of the tree of many branches."

Saskatoon berries handily replaced currants at the Christmas meal.

The aforementioned berry is the main ingredient in saskatoon pie. This is not an observation worthy of Sherlock Holmes. The pie itself, though, is worthy of anyone. Odds are that it was the dessert featured in an oft-repeated Prairie anecdote. The story has been told many times, but it's hard to find a written account. It may be an urban legend or, more properly, a rural myth, but here it is. It seems that several decades ago a member of the British royal family wanted to visit an authentic Prairie farm. A farmhouse was chosen, and the visit was worked into the royal itinerary. The farmwife prepared a typical country meal. As she cleared the supper plates, she offered some advice that her pampered guest had surely never heard before: "Save your fork, Prince, there's pie!"

The only exclusively native cereal in Canada is wild rice. It appears in the swampier sections of northern Saskatchewan. It's especially plentiful in Manitoba, particularly in the Whiteshell and Nopiming Provincial Park areas. Wild rice was the only cereal consumed by First Nations prior to Samuel de Champlain's arrival in Quebec in 1608. It was used in many First Nations foods, including bread. It added some variety to the menus of the first explorers in the west. The stalks grow as high as just under 2.5 metres and yield dark-husked kernels. Like basmati, wild rice has a distinct nutlike flavour. Don't overcook it; it should come off the fork crunchy.

Victual Rituals

The Christmas Eve meal is more than just a great eat. Orthodox denominations, such as Ukrainian Catholics, that follow the old Julian calendar recognize January 7 as Christ's birthday. Whether it's on December 24 or January 6, their Christmas Eve meal is loaded with ceremony. For a start, it isn't served until the first star is visible in the sky. Christ's disciples are represented by 12 meatless dishes. The supper table is the manger, so straw is placed under the tablecloth. A candle is placed in *kolach*, a round, braided bread, to recognize Christ as the light of the world and the bread of life. The first dish served is *kutia*, made up of boiled wheat with honey, nuts, and poppy seeds.

The Plains Cree honoured their late ancestors on Flower Day, a late-August ceremony, by burning sweetgrass (which is still burned in many Native ceremonies) and by dining near the graves on a soup made from dried meat and herbal tea. On other occasions, a guest portioned off a bit of food from his or her plate and put it in a small container as an offering to Manitou. The huge feast held to conclude the Plains Cree's Sun Dance festival always included dried chokecherry paste and saskatoon berries.

Another common "berry" is the cackleberry, better known as the egg.

Food played an important role in the "sodding bees" that were common as settlers first tamed the land. When a newcomer arrived, neighbours came to help build a sod house and barn. If enough people chipped in, the tough job was done in a day. The women provided the men with the fuel that they needed to complete their labours, and they ensured that the sodding bee was a social gathering as well as a functional one. They brought meat, bread, desserts, and more. At the end of the day, someone usually brought out a fiddle, and labour gave way to leisure.

Table Manners

Early ranches found a novel way to serve large groups in their dining halls. A makeshift lazy Susan was constructed from a buggy wheel — topped with a flat wood surface — and mounted into the table. The idea is credited to Fred Anderson, a cook at the Oxley Ranch, northwest of Fort Macleod.

101

One time when Albertan farmwife Ellen Liveley prepared lunch for a crew of farm workers, one of the normally respectful men refused to take his hat off when he sat down at the table. She later learned that the man had caught a field mouse to feed to his cat. He needed to keep the mouse alive until he got home, so he imprisoned the unlucky rodent under his cap.

The Depression shaped not only what was on the supper table but also the behaviour of those seated around it. For example, it created the phrase "bread and point." People pointed their knives at the butter dish if they wanted butter. When there wasn't any, which was often, they pointed to no avail. "Bread and point" became a pseudonym for dry bread.

 **A 1997 survey found that 50 percent of beef sold by weight in Canada is ground beef, compared with 21 percent steak and 18 percent roast.**

There was no manners guide for the first cowboys, but there was an understood code of conduct when it came to dining. No one approached the cook with plate in hand until the cook signalled that dinner was served. No one went for seconds until everyone had obtained a first serving. Hats were acceptable unless a woman was present. The cowboys had one habit that's still useful today: when eating outside in the rain, push your hat back on your head so that the water rolls back off the brim rather than forward onto your plate.

Not Exactly Fine China

It was possible, in the 1870s, to be served food from a chamber pot. Reginald Berry found this out when, as a representative for the Hudson's Bay Company, he attended a Narive feast near Cumberland House in northeastern Saskatchewan. After diplomatically talking his way out of a helping of dog meat, he was served saskatoon berries in the all-too-familiar pot. He was spared the mistake of offending his hosts when it was explained to him that the HBC's clerk at Cumberland House had recently played a trick on a French fur trader by sending him 144 chamber pots instead of the one that he had ordered. It's hard to understand why the trader accepted the costly order, but he turned it to his advantage. The trader simply told local Natives that the pots were the latest table dish and traded them for furs.

Breadbasket of the World

The Prairie region, and Saskatchewan in particular, likes to refer to itself as "the breadbasket of the world." In fact, the biggest single consumer of Canadian wheat is Canada, but when you add up all the other nations eager to buy our product it's clear that Canadian agriculture is export-oriented. We sell roughly twice as much wheat as we consume, almost all of it grown in the three Prairie provinces. China has traditionally been our biggest customer of wheat other than durum, although Iran recently took top spot when it bought two million tonnes in 1996-97. The most encouraging development in agriculture has been diversification of crops, a lesson learned after debt, drought, and low prices hammered many a wheat farmer during the 1980s. Farmers are reserving spaces in their fields to grow specialty crops such as chickpeas or lucrative canola. The 1990s have also seen the growth of Prairie-based food production: agricultural crops once transported east and west to be turned into foodstuffs are now remaining here to be processed and packaged.

Wheat had been grown across Europe, Asia, and Africa for thousands of years before it appeared in North America in the late 15th century. The two main cultivated species today are common wheat (for bread and pastry flours and breakfast cereals) and durum (for pasta). From 1800 to 1860, wheat varieties that had proved successful in England were sent to Canada to see which ones would "take." The Hudson's Bay Company operated several experimental farms in Manitoba in an effort to identify a strain that would bring self-sufficiency to those first settlers. The settlers did some experimenting of their own too: between 1860 and 1890, they introduced 28 different wheat varieties.

In 1994 canola surpassed wheat as the most valuable crop in Canada.

Scottish settlers brought wheat to western Canada and achieved limited success at the Red River Settlement. However, growing wheat remained a tricky proposition: the seed that fed European families simply wasn't made for a Canadian winter. Scots-born Ontario farmer David Fife spent years trying to develop a strain of wheat well-suited to his new country. In 1843 a friend mailed him some seeds from Europe. Only one of the seeds resulted in a healthy stalk. Fife planted the seeds from that stalk and came up with Red Fife. It was more resistant to disease, produced a high yield, and made excellent bread. It also matured 10 days sooner than other strains — an important quality in regions with prolonged winters and short growing seasons. Red Fife's popularity across the Prairies was helped greatly when the strain was awarded first prize at the Winnipeg Exhibition's contest for Manitoba-grown wheat.

Whisky Coulee was named after an early still.

Federal agricultural researcher Charles Saunders made a good thing better in 1907 by crossing Fife's strain with Hard Red Calcutta, from India. The resulting hybrid was ready for harvest just 100 days after it was sown. Don't underestimate the importance of shaving a few weeks off the growing time. Doing so meant that the new wheat — called Marquis — could be planted in more northerly areas, thereby expanding the arable land on the Prairies. By 1920 more than six million hectares of Prairie soil grew Marquis wheat. Both it and Red Fife are varieties of hard red spring wheat — the best anywhere.

Saskatchewan's Seager Wheeler was the Michael Jordan of wheat. He won top prize (and 1,000 bucks) for the best North American hard spring wheat at a fair in New York in 1911. Wheeler, known as the wheat wizard, went on to win the same award four more times. The W. Seager Wheeler Farm, located about six kilometres east of Rosthern, includes a museum dedicated to Wheeler.

We take wheat pretty seriously around here. So seriously, in fact, that Regina councillors repeatedly drafted bylaws to ensure that local bakers didn't go against the grain. The first was passed in 1885 and stated "That the size of Baker's Bread for this town shall be the loaf weighing four pounds and the half weighing two pounds: and no person shall sell or dispose of any loaf of any other size or weight." The fine for defying the bylaw was no less than $1 and no more than $50. Remarkably, this was only the 17th bylaw in the town's history, suggesting that the town fathers were a bit short of things to worry about. In 1918, perhaps recognizing that the original bylaw called for one heck of a big loaf of bread, council passed a new bylaw that stipulated 20-ounce loaves. The fine was hiked to $100. Rolls had to weigh between one and two ounces each, "and said rolls shall be baked in a pan, and not on the oven bottom."

The Pretty Crop with the Ugly Name

Actually we call it canola now, and there's no mistaking it. No other agricultural crop produces anything like the bright blast of yellow that crowns land seeded with canola, once known as rapeseed. The original name comes from *rapum*, the Latin word for "turnip," a cousin of canola. Although Asian people had grown it for its edible oil for 4,000 years, it wasn't planted in Canada until World War II, and only then as a lubricant for marine engines. The seed was too acidic and just plain awful-tasting to eat.

It took decades of refinement in the lab and the field before the plant's promise was recognized and exploited. In Canada and Europe, the tiny hard-shelled seed is crushed to yield an oil used for cooking, margarine, and salad dressing. Once the oil is extracted, the remaining meal is used as a high-protein livestock feed. In the 1970s, the industry settled on the name canola — a spin on "Canadian oil." In the health-conscious 1990s, it has become a highly profitable crop that has bumped wheat from many fields. In 1994 Canadian canola production peaked at 5.7 million hectares and has held steady since.

Cowboys frequently had a hankering for hot rocks.
They also liked sinkers. And belly busters.
And dough gods. All of which are
one and the same. Biscuits!

World's Best Corn

The town of Taber, in south-central Alberta, is known for one thing: corn. I've met people in Taber who roll their eyes at the very mention of "Taber corn" and protest that the identity of their community has been reduced to a vegetable. Their protest is understandable; nonetheless, Taber corn is just about the best-tasting vegetable anywhere in the world. There are several varieties of Taber corn, each differing in colour, length of growing season, and taste. For example, corn with a longer growing season yields plumper, sweeter kernels. Corn producers advise consumers to pick cobs that feel cooler than those around them because the quality of sweet corn declines in warmer temperatures. Thus, store the cobs in a cool place. According to former mayor Harley Phillips, the fields that surround his town for 24 kilometres in each direction benefit from exactly the right combination of soil, irrigation, and sunlight. The result is a corn containing three teaspoons of sugar per cob. "I don't recommend it for diabetics," Phillips cautions.

Raising Our Glasses

The Depression made penny-pinchers out of everyone. Thanks to a few enterprising, if not exactly law-abiding, citizens, it was possible to reduce one's liquor bills. Many an innocent-looking home had its own still. Neighbours were known to come knocking on the door with an empty beer bottle and, a few coins later, leaving with a full one.

The recipe called for potatoes or some other food that would ferment. The food was boiled, strained, and then left to ferment. The alcohol was separated through distillation and left to sit some more. Then it was a matter of finding something to add to the alcohol to make it a bit more palatable. The only difference between this concoction and unleaded petroleum is that one is a flammable, poisonous liquid capable of propelling an automobile and the other is gasoline.

Suet, the fat around the bovine kidney, used to be a common substitute for butter and lard.

There really was such a thing as firewater. It was the evil stuff that (primarily) American whisky traders gave to Plains Indians at the unscrupulous exchange rate of one buffalo hide per cup. In 1899 Lethbridge druggist John Higinbotham recorded the ghastly recipe:
- one quart of medicinal alcohol
- one bottle of Jamaican ginger
- one quart of black molasses
- one pound of chewing tobacco (I'm going to be sick)
- boil in water.

Here's about as simple a cocktail as you can mix. This lowball highball is called a Calgary Redeye: one part beer, one part tomato juice. Write that down so you don't forget it.

On the Prairies, the best-known of the new wave of "microbreweries" is Calgary's Big Rock Brewery. Founder Ed McNally had a logical reason for putting his own brew on tap in 1985. He liked beer, but not what was commercially available. Using a meticulous German method of brewing, McNally's plant produced a line of ales, porters, and other beers so popular that Big Rock eventually became too big to be considered a true microbrewery (no more than 1.44 million dozen bottles a year).

Others have followed in McNally's footsteps. Bow Valley Brewing opened in 1995 in Canmore and quickly won a gold medal at the International World Beer Cup competition.

Or, if You Prefer Milk ...

Alberta produced a world champion in Alcarta Gerben. She's not a household name, but she's a legend in the dairy industry. Alcarta Gerben was a cow, an amazingly productive one. Calgary cattleman Harry Hays bought the Holstein and, recognizing her superior attributes, submitted her to a year-long, government-supervised production test in 1944. While the cow was fed and milked for 365 days, Hays had his eye on the world record for annual butterfat production, set by a U.S. cow at 1,402 pounds. When the test was finished, Alcarta Gerben had produced 27,748 pounds of milk and a new world-record 1,409 pounds of butterfat (equal to 1,716 pounds of butter). When the cow's achievement was toasted at Hays's celebratory party, the guests lifted glasses full of Alcarta Gerben's best.

The prairie chicken is a game bird common in Manitoba. Marinate, then cook.

When coffee was in short supply, settlers found a substitute in what was probably the first place they looked — the field. Wheat or barley was used in place of coffee. It had to be ground down and then cooked slightly in a low oven. Once browned, it was ground again, perhaps with chicory for additional flavour.

You Eat *What?*

- Isaac Stringer, in his duties as a bishop and then as archbishop of Rupert's Land, travelled extensively through the Manitoba wilderness. On one such occasion, he became lost in the woods for 51 days before he reached an Inuit camp. The bishop found a food source close at hand — or, rather, at foot. He boiled his rawhide boots. In his diary, he remarked that the result was "palatable." Two days later, he wrote that he was still eating boot but complained that it wasn't enough. It's too bad that he didn't have bigger feet — he could have prepared larger portions.

- The Battleford newspaper ran an article in 1890 advocating the gopher as a suitable source of protein when other meats were scarce. Fried gopher legs were not unheard of, after all. Had the paper's advice been heeded, no one would have gone hungry on the Prairies. Apparently most of us would rather risk hunger than eat a rodent.

- The past and present king of all strange Prairie food is the prairie oyster. If you don't already know what it is, then you probably don't want to know. Prairie oysters have also been called calves' fries. Here's the recipe. First, remove the calf's testicles. Second, return the animal to the field for a life that will now be both shorter and far less happy. Third, soak the testicles in salted water; clean them; dip them in egg, milk, and bread crumbs; and fry them in oil. (Serve them with saskatoons for people who like nuts and berries.)

But wait a minute, a prairie oyster is also a drink. Just add one egg to a pint of beer. The egg should be raw. And unshelled.

Here's another definition, one that appeared during the 1930s when a customer at a diner had more hunger than money. The key was that the ingredients were all condiments laid out for free on the counter or table. First, take a soda cracker and form a small retaining wall of butter along its edges. Pour some ketchup in the centre. The butter rim should keep it in place. Eat it as you would an oyster — in one bite. As Canada's economy peaks and plummets, we can rest assured that things really aren't so bad as long as this particular form of prairie oyster remains a memory.

 **Before the turkey became the most common Yuletide meal, goose, duck, and prairie chicken were each a popular main course.**

Wes Gidluck, a farmer from near Biggar, Saskatchewan, was recognized as the country's ultimate Kraft Dinner diner. As a result of his passion for the pasta, he won prize money and one box of Kraft Dinner for every day of 1999. His picture also appeared on three million boxes of the noodles.

108

Ask for It by Name

What is it that makes the phrase "Alberta beef" an assurance of quality? It's nothing mysterious, according to Fred Free, a regional meat consultant with Cargill Foods.

Wheat grown in a dry climate like that of the Prairies produces flour with a high protein content.

"They genetically made the cattle pretty good. They've bred the cattle to get marbling into the meat, which is your tenderness. They bred them to reach maturity at a very young age," says Fred. "It's tender, because it's younger. They feed the cattle differently. In the Prairies, all your cattle are finished with barley and wheat." Calves still eat a lot of grass for the first year after weaning, but they spend their final 100 days before slaughter dining on barley and wheat. Another advantage is that Alberta cattle don't have to travel far from the finishing barns to Cargill's meat-packing plants in centrally located High River. Health-conscious consumers who turned away from beef should consider that it is now 50 percent leaner and has 34 percent fewer calories than it did 20 years ago.

Chapter 6

How We Have Fun

THE HUNTERS: THE ONLY GAME IN TOWN

Lorne Hunter walks into the kitchen of his southwest Saskatchewan farmhouse, and suddenly he's wearing a second coat. It's Brock, his 10-year-old son, who has launched himself upward into his father's arms. Lorne hugs him back. He hasn't seen Brock in a few days. Then it's over to the couch, where a formerly mobile 15-year-old lays stretched out, his broken left shin wrapped and elevated. This is Dusty, the second son. He gets a hug too.

"That's the worst of it, and the biggest fear of any parent," Lorne says as he sits down to a coffee. "My kids are always coming home with slashed shins and sprained fingers." He nods in Dusty's direction. "This is the first major injury we've suffered in the family."

The family: Lorne and Norma Hunter, an assortment of pets, and five sons. Sons who wear skates as often as they wear shoes. Four of them play hockey. The fifth must wait two more years for his seventh birthday before he'll be allowed to join an organized team, a family rule.

For many Prairie kids, the national pastime is the only sport worth playing. Almost every town, even the smallest, has an arena or rink. If not, then the one down the road does. And no other sport is as organized, with so many teams, leagues, and tournaments. Hockey is ingrained into small-town Prairie culture.

The Hunters run a pretty big farm a few kilometres south of Shaunavon. Lorne grew up here, skating on the backyard rink that his father built. With his youthful good looks and thick hair grown long at the back, Lorne looks less like a grain farmer than the professional figure skater he used to be. And Norma, slender and energetic, with long dark hair, looks far too young to have had five children.

The oldest is J. J. The 17-year-old has been listed by the Melfort Mustangs of the Saskatchewan Junior Hockey League (SJHL) — essentially put on a waiting list. Dusty is next. Both are fast, skilled players. Dusty has also been listed by an SJHL team, although that's a bittersweet achievement. Barely 24 hours earlier, he was showing his stuff at a recruitment camp hosted by the Kindersley Clippers. He was punctuating his performance with another fast skate down the ice when several things went wrong at once. An opponent cross-checked him from behind. Then his skate hit a rut, trapping his foot, and his shinbone snapped cleanly in half. Several hours later, he learned that the Clippers had listed him. The team will have the right of first refusal if he advances to junior hockey from the midget league. If his leg heals.

After Dusty comes Luke. The 12-year-old is perhaps the best of the lot, his dad observes. For one thing, he's filling out at an earlier age. That helps in hockey. Especially when you're a Hunter with a reputation that brings out the gunslinger in other young players. Then comes Brock, an unlikely looking jock in his round glasses and slight frame. Then Ty, waiting for his seventh birthday. This is Team Hunter.

The Hunters acknowledge that the sport they share doesn't always share them. "From a family perspective, it's probably more detrimental than it is a coagulator," Lorne says. "You can no longer do things together ... Two years ago, we were with seven hockey teams. That's just the oldest four boys." At the time, Dusty played on a Swift Current team 112 kilometres away. "Thursday mornings, he was up at 4 a.m. to get to hockey practice and then get back for school," Norma says. Which meant that she, as chauffeur, was also up then.

112

What's impressive — or perhaps bewildering — is that hockey isn't the Hunters' sole passion. "I had seen one hockey game before I married Lorne," Norma says. Her love was music. So, years ago, she struck a bargain with her husband. Hockey would be something for him to enjoy with the boys (she likely hadn't foreseen the many hours that she was destined to spend inside hockey rinks), and she would encourage them in music. The boys tackled it with comparable zeal, so that now Lorne and Norma are not only one goalie short of a starting lineup but also one drummer short of a sextet.

There are at least two dozen skates stored in the basement, onetime tools turned into spent mementos. This type of hand-me-down only goes so far. The Hunters could build their own arena with the wood from all the sticks that their sons have worn out. The total bill over the past 10 years has a lot of zeros. "I don't keep track on purpose," Lorne says of the money. "Because I don't want to know." He smiles.

For all the time and money they've invested, the Hunters are surprisingly realistic about the returns. Sure, they hope that the boys will advance to the SJHL, which in turn might lead to college scholarships in the United States. Then there's the better-known forum for junior hockey, the Western Hockey League. It's the path that most often leads to the big leagues. For all their talk about hockey, though, three letters are seemingly absent from the Hunters' vocabulary: NHL.

Curling is so Prairie that W. O. Mitchell wrote a play about it (*The Black Bonspiel of Wullie MacCrimmon*).

At the mere mention of professional hockey, mom and dad shake their heads. "We don't have stars in our eyes," Norma says. "There are people who are obsessed with the sport," Lorne says. "They're determined their kids are going to play pro." He describes one father who had his five-year-old lifting weights and dieting. For Lorne and Norma, encouraging their sons in hockey is not about raising the next Eric Lindros. And, despite the many pleasures that it brings the boys and them, it imposes burdens that would buckle many parents.

So, why? "It starts so innocent," Lorne says. He's standing in what used to be J. J.'s bedroom, surrounded by at least a dozen trophies and twice as many medals.

"You're out with the little guy, and you say, 'I'm going to teach J. J. how to skate.' Lo and behold, J. J. is doing pretty good at that. We might as well put him in hockey. The first thing you know, here comes little J. J., and he wins the scoring. Then Dusty comes along and sees his big brother playing hockey, and, well, we better teach him too.

"And then there's two-year-old Luke, watching the scoreboard during his brothers' games, always asking his dad when he can play. 'Try and tell that kid he can't play hockey.' "

The number of kids who eventually get to lace 'em up for an NHL team is tiny. Occasionally a young man emerges from the crowded junior leagues and graduates to the pros, likely for a short, unspectacular career. How, then, do we explain the Sutter boys? Six of the seven sons raised on a farm near Viking, Alberta, have played in the NHL, and two of them have played on championship teams. The trend started when Brian put on a St. Louis jersey in 1976. He was followed by Darryl, Duane, Brent, Ron, and Rich. For nearly a quarter-century, there has been at least one Sutter playing Canada's game. As the brothers hang up the skates to take on coaching and other off-ice duties, their sons (and daughters) are preparing to crack the big leagues.

Kelvington, Saskatchewan, calls itself "the Hockey Factory" because of the many hockey players whom it has produced. Wendel Clark, for one, grew up there.

Hockey Heroes

One of the toughest superstars to ever lace up skates came from the unlikely sounding town of Floral, Saskatchewan. Make fun of Gordie Howe's hometown at your own peril. One of his peers once remarked that "Howe was tougher than a night in jail." He played on four championship teams during his 25 seasons with the Detroit Red Wings. He came back from retirement in 1979 to play one season with the Hartford Whalers. He retired again with several NHL regular-season records, including games played (1,767) and points (1,850). Howe was recognized as both the league's top scorer and its most valuable player six times. Amazingly, on October 3, 1997, the 69-year-old played a single shift lasting 40 seconds for the IHL Detroit Vipers to become the only player to play professional hockey over six decades.

Only three years after Bryan Trottier won the Calder Trophy for rookie of the year, he had his dream season. In 1978-79, the New York Islander piled up 134 points and won the Hart (most valuable player) and Art Ross (most points) Trophies. The next year, the lad from Val Marie, Saskatchewan, won the Conn Smythe Trophy as the most valuable player in the playoffs. He played on six Stanley Cup teams during his 18 seasons, four with the New York Islanders and two with the Pittsburgh Penguins.

The first Mounted Police who crossed the Prairies and built Fort Macleod in southwestern Alberta bowled, curled, fenced, and played lacrosse, polo, and cricket to relieve the inevitable boredom.

Imagine scoring three goals in 21 seconds. Chicago Black Hawk Bill Mosienko did so against the New York Rangers on March 23, 1952. Nearly 50 years later, no one has come close to matching the Winnipeg native's machine gun-like burst of productivity. After retiring from hockey, he moved back to Winnipeg and opened the Mosienko Lanes bowling alley on Main Street.

Another Winnipeg boy is remembered as one of the greatest goalies to ever patrol the crease. In 1974 Terry Sawchuk was named Manitoba's hockey player of the century. He was rookie of the year in 1951 when he started with the Detroit Red Wings. He moved to the Maple Leafs and blocked enough shots to give Toronto its last Stanley Cup, way back in 1967. His career records of 103 shutouts and 447 wins still stand. Sawchuk died under unusual circumstances in his home in New York state in 1970.

Glenn Hall's St. Louis Blues lost the 1968 Stanley Cup series, but the goalie won the Conn Smythe Trophy for postseason play by allowing only 11 of 151 shots past him during the four-game series. It was one of many awards won by "Mr. Goalie." Born in Humboldt, Saskatchewan, Hall played 16 years in the NHL. He won the Calder Trophy as top rookie, led the league in shutouts over six seasons, and three times beat all other goalies for the Vezina Trophy. He was netminder when the Chicago Black Hawks won the Stanley Cup in 1961.

Mark Messier combines terrific skills with a bruising on-ice presence that made him an indispensable cog in the Oilers machine that won five

115

championships (the last one without buddy Wayne Gretzky, who had been traded to the L.A. Kings). The centre from Edmonton took his game to New York, where he captained the Rangers to their first Stanley Cup in 54 years. After a brief whistlestop in Vancouver, the frequent all-star is now back in New York playing for the Rangers.

 **At five foot six, Theoren Fleury was supposed to be too small to play in the NHL. That's why the Oxbow, Saskatchewan, product went 166th in the 1987 draft. Since then, he's played in seven all-star games.**

The best female hockey player in the world first tied her skates in Shaunavon, Saskatchewan. Hayley Wickenheiser has scored four gold medals (and many more goals) playing for Canada's national team in the Women's World Hockey Championships. She earned a silver medal when the Canadian women lost to the U.S. at the Winter Olympics in Nagano, Japan, in 1998. Four years later, she captained the team that returned to beat the Americans and win gold at the Salt Lake City Olympics. Then she made history. Hayley cracked the lineup of Kirkkonummen Salamat, a Finnish men's team, and, on January 11, 2003, she became the first woman to score a goal in a men's professional game. Her greatest achievement may be the example she has set for girls around the world. More and more hockey fans are hearing announcers exclaim "She shoots, she scores!"

Each of the three biggest Prairie cities has hosted an NHL team, but Winnipeg wasn't able to hold on to its maybe-next-year Jets, who ended two decades of futility by moving to Phoenix in 1996. The Calgary Flames have been more successful. Since moving from Atlanta in 1980, they won the Stanley Cup in 1989 and, for a time, boasted the most memorable moustache in professional sports — team captain Lanny McDonald's red horse tails. Of course, the best NHL team from the Prairies — one of the greatest ever — was the Edmonton Oilers, who won five championships between 1984 and 1990.

The Canadian team that won the first-ever gold medal for hockey at the 1920 Olympic Games in Antwerp, Belgium, was comprised of second-generation Canadians from an Icelandic neighbourhood in Winnipeg's west end. Year after year, these neighbourhood lads played on a team called the Falcons and were strong enough in 1920 to be selected to represent the entire country. The Falcons cruised through most of their games before beating the U.S. team 2-0 in front of a gleeful pro-Falcon crowd.

Some college students will do anything to avoid a midterm. In April 1971, the Pancakes and the Eagles waged the longest nonprofessional hockey game ever, at Calgary's Mount Royal College. After 56 hours, 19 minutes, and 45 seconds, the Pancakes won 462-425. Had Don Cherry been the commentator, even he would have run out of things to say.

WINTER FUN; OR, YOU DON'T HAVE TO BE BRAIN-DEAD, BUT IT HELPS

Ice fishers such as Larry Gnius — the truly ardent ones who are only too happy to spend a frigid Saturday sitting atop a frozen lake — defend their pastime with talk about camaraderie, winter's chilly splendour, and the familiar glee of actually pulling in a fish.

The rest of us are more inclined to wonder, "What are they thinking?" It's not like most Prairie people don't get enough of the cold. Ice fishing also sounds a tad, well, dull. The middle guys in a four-man bobsled have more to do.

"It's kind of a social thing. You see the same people, and you're talking to each other, asking how you're doing," says Gnius (pronounced ga-*noose*; according to Larry, who's from Regina, he's the last Gnius in the world). "You'll go out and see a guy who maybe in town you only see once a year, and out there you'll see him three times. By winter's end, you realize you've made 50 acquaintances, and 49 and a half are likable people." It helps to forge these simple bonds, because it never hurts to have someone you can count on phone you on days when the fish are biting and you're still sleeping.

Larry doesn't even use a shack for shelter. He's out there on the ice, from sunrise to sunset, moving between the dozens of holes that he's drilled for the day. He's got his Thermos, his lunch, and maybe a folding chair. The closest that he gets to indoors is the cab of his truck, which he drives right out onto the ice. It's not unusual for him to set up a camp stove on the lowered tailgate and cook his catch right there. He believes that walleye and perch caught in winter make for better eating. Although a fattened four-kilogram summer walleye looks impressive, a one-kilogram winter specimen is tastier, he says.

Saskatchewan's ice fishing season extends from early December to late March. To the outsider, this stretch of year makes for one obvious disadvantage.

"Aren't you cold?" I ask on the phone.

"Just get used to it," Larry responds. "Most of the winter, I walk around

117

without gloves. I don't know if it's a blessing or not. I'm brain-dead. I don't feel the cold."

Largely because of the wintry setting, ice fishing will forever remain a lesser-known pastime, with only slightly more enthusiasts than, say, cow-tipping. According to Larry, the last Gnius, that's just fine. He likes that still winter air. "You don't hear people. You just sit there and think a lot and let the world go by."

There must be a reason why one province has produced the two greatest curling rinks ever. In the 1958-59 season, the Richardson rink of brothers Ernie and Garnet ("Sam") and cousins Arnold and Wes, from Stoughton, Saskatchewan, relied on their aggressive take-out play to post a 45-3 record. And they became the youngest team ever to win the Brier. They won four Briers over five years and four world championships.

Nearly 40 years later, Regina's Sandra Peterson rink (and, one marriage later, the Sandra Schmirler rink) proved to be the most successful women's squad ever. After capturing the national title, Schmirler's curlers — Sandra, Jan Betker, Joan McCusker, Marcia Gudereit, and fifth Anita Ford — won the first back-to-back women's world curling championships in 1993 and 1994. They continued to play well even as they underwent some changes, including some marriages, some babies, and Anita handing over the role of fifth to her daughter, Atina. In 1997 the new version captured the provincial, national, and world championships all over again. The women capped off these victories in marvellous style by winning the first-ever gold medal for curling at the 1998 Winter Olympics at Nagano, Japan. The curling world shed tears in 2000 when Sandra died of cancer at age 36.

Calgarians might dispute the Richardsons' claim. One of their own, Ron Northcott, skipped a rink to the Canadian and world titles in 1966, 1968, and 1969. Northcott's rink hailed from Vulcan.

Swinging in the Summer

When Jason Zuback takes aim at a tee and swings, he's not trying for a hole in one. He's aiming for a hole in the ozone layer. The pharmacist from Drayton Valley, Alberta, can drive a golf ball farther than anyone else on the planet. Zuback won the Re/Max North American Long Drive Championship in 1996 and successfully took on all challengers in 1997. In 1992 the young man hit a ball an astounding 466 metres (511 yards) on the fourth hole of the Land o' Lakes course at Coaldale, Alberta. The muscular golfer sent one ball 653 metres (714 yards) down an airport runway. From close range, Zuback can drive a golf ball through a copy of the Edmonton *Yellow Pages*. There may not be much call for that skill in the workforce, but it's impressive nonetheless.

"No service will be provided at this bar to any Calgarian on a horse" — sign in Hotel Vancouver during the 1971 Grey Cup.

"I'M GOING GOLFING, HONEY.
SEE YOU NEXT MONTH."
Grant Painter knows how to raise money. He just can't seem to raise it in a normal way. The business-systems sales rep from Calgary is known for staging record-breaking, grin-inducing fundraisers. As Stampederman, he helped the CFL club to sell 1994 season tickets by living in a tent for seven days on a 15-metre-high scaffold. As Lawnmower Man the following year, he raised money for the Boys and Girls Club by pushing a mower for a world record six days from Edmonton to Calgary.

On September 28, 1996, Painter completed his most imaginative scheme when he drained a putt on the Paisley Golf Oasis. By that time calling himself Golfman, he and three friends golfed an 18-hole course that started on the Target Green Golf Centre in Calgary and continued across farmers' fields and alongside the Trans-Canada Highway before ending at the Paisley course west of Regina. That's right: the back nine were in a whole other province. This time the beneficiary was cancer research. It took two weeks for the foursome to play the 600-kilometre course. (Not bad, although I've played almost as long on a regular 18-hole golf course.) If he ever repeats the feat, he'll no doubt be looking to take a few hundred strokes off his game.

The Gateway Cities Golf Course straddles the Saskatchewan-Montana border. As a result, the ninth hole occupies two different time zones.

Three Cheers for Three-Down Football
For five decades, Canadian fans have shouted themselves hoarse over the play of Canadian and American athletes who banged helmets and broke tackles in the Canadian Football League. Three-down football gets little respect outside Canada, but it is appreciated in its homeland, especially across the Prairies.

Saskatchewan Roughrider fans, who usually have less to cheer about than fans of the Jamaican bobsled team, look back reverently to the 1960s and 1970s when quarterback Ron "the Little General" Lancaster, fullback George Reed, and the guys in the trenches kept the team competitive and brought it one of its few Grey Cup victories in 1966.

"The Bud Grant era" was the height of glory for the Winnipeg Blue Bombers, who won the Grey Cup in 1958, 1959, 1961, and 1962. Coach Grant and quarterback Ken Ploen were the heart of the franchise.

 **According to a *Maclean's* and CBC poll conducted in 1998, only 12 percent of Prairie residents considered themselves "very sexually active" — the lowest percentage of any region in the country.**

When the Calgary Stampeders won their first Grey Cup in 1948, they proved that the long-outclassed western teams were ready to compete with the strong eastern clubs. More than that, the high-spirited boosterism of the Calgary fans created a Canadian tradition: a weeklong celebration at each Grey Cup. The most famous member of the Stamps was Wayne Harris, who played from 1961 to 1972. He was nicknamed "the Thumper," and a number of quarterbacks knew why. The middle linebacker was the CFL's outstanding lineman four times.

But no Prairie football team deserves the term "dynasty" more than the Edmonton Eskimos of 1978 to 1982. They won the Grey Cup each of those five years, due largely to the howitzer arm of signal caller Warren Moon, one of the few CFL superstars to continue his success in the NFL.

The Edmonton Eskimos couldn't take a home crowd to the 1952 Grey Cup game against the Argonauts in Toronto, so they took a home meal. According to the *Toronto Star*, the Eskimo players brought Edmonton water in special containers and flew in Alberta bread and beef. This tactic didn't help. The Argos won.

There's something about the way in which the Prairies throw a party that sets us apart, and nothing exemplifies this difference better than our Grey Cup celebrations. We're gracious and keen hosts, excited that you came, determined that you have a good time. Look at the various Grey Cup festivities that have been held in each of the four CFL cities across the Prairies. Every business, bar, and restaurant is touched by the fervour. During the Grey Cup weekend itself, each day opens with pancake breakfasts and closes with benign drunkenness. It's a Molson's commercial come to life.

Now compare the atmosphere prevalent in the more reserved, oh-so-cosmopolitan Grey Cup cities such as Toronto and Vancouver. Seats go unsold. Those bigger centres sometimes behave as if the league, its players, and the fans should feel fortunate for being allowed to converge in them. In the Prairie cities, the big game is the only game in town.

Good Sports

Dr. James Naismith called the Edmonton Grads the finest basketball team to ever play the game. That's pretty high praise coming from the guy who invented the sport. The all-woman Commercial Graduates Basketball Club began as the school team for McDougall Commercial High School and was composed of students or alumnae throughout the team's 25-year career. Between 1915 and 1940, the Grads won 93 percent of their games and 108 titles, from local and national championships (which they completely dominated) to international competitions (during three European tours, they didn't lose a game).

The first "stampede" anywhere was held in Raymond, Alberta, in 1902.

There were few female trapshooters who could challenge Susan Nattrass, so the Edmonton shooter set her sights on her own achievements. She won the 1974 world championship by shooting a record 143 out of 150 points. The next year, she won another world title and set another record. And in 1977. And in 1978. In 1979 she won her fifth world title in six years.

A little guy from Taber, Alberta, was the $25 million man. Jockey Johnny Longden won his first horse race in 1928. He retired in 1966 with a then-record 6,032 career victories and had ridden horses to $24,665,800 in prize money. Longden was the first North American jockey to win 4,000 races and was crowned the world's top jockey three times.

Can you name an athlete so dominant that she won the world championship six years in a row, from 1988 to 1993? Her name is Stacy Singer, and, if her sport were basketball or figure skating, she'd be hawking running shoes or her own line of cosmetics. But Stacy's sport was baton twirling. At the age of eight, Stacy, from Regina, became the youngest Canadian twirler to compete at the world championship, where she won gold in the junior class, beating girls as much as five years older. From 1985 until her retirement in 1993, she placed first at every provincial and national freestyle twirling competition.

John Ware, reputed to be Canada's first black cowboy, was nicknamed "the Smoked Irishman."

Olympic glory famously eluded Kurt Browning, but that was the only goal that he couldn't reach when he put skates on. In 1988, a month after his eighth-place finish at his first Olympic Games, Browning became the first figure skater to manage a quadruple jump in competition. From Caroline, Alberta, he was the Canadian and world champion from 1989 to 1991.

Sylvia Burka started scorching the ice as a girl in Winnipeg and would go on to win the junior world speed skating championship in 1973. She graduated to the adult competition and won the world championships in 1976 and 1977. She won an amazing 21 world speed skating titles and finished fourth at the 1976 Olympic Games in Montreal.

But that's not all. Burka was a two-sport champion. In 1980 and 1982, she set world record times in the 1,000-metre women's cycling race. Small wonder that she was named Manitoba's female athlete of the year six times.

Rueben Mayes was "the Saint from North Battleford." The running back has been the most successful Prairie export to the NFL, where he ran for 1,353 yards during his rookie season with the New Orleans Saints in 1986.

As anyone who has driven through small Prairie towns in summer knows, the national pastime of the United States is pretty popular up here too. Terry Puhl, a Melville, Saskatchewan, lad, played 15 years of pro baseball, most of them with the Houston Astros. He played more games (1,531) and has more hits (1,361) than any other Canadian. He also set a National League record for batting average in a league championship series by hitting .526 in 1980. Remarkably he made only 18 errors in his career, giving him the major-league record for fielding percentage by an outfielder: .993!

Swimmer Mark Tewksbury was just eight years old when he joined Calgary's Cascade Club. By the time that he moved on, he had set numerous club records, several of which still stand. Breaking records in the pool became a bit of a habit for him. In 1992 he swam to a world record time of 52.5 seconds in the short-course 100-metre backstroke. The same year, he won a gold medal and set an Olympic record in the 100-metre backstroke with a time of 53.98 seconds.

In 1988 Calgary's Carolyn Waldo won the solo synchronized swimming event and, with partner Michelle Cameron, the duet competition, making her the first Canadian woman to win two gold medals at a single Olympic Games. The medals capped a decade of medal-winning performances in synchronized swimming competitions.

It is satisfying whenever a Prairie athlete succeeds in a water sport. Colleen Miller virtually ruled women's rowing in the early 1990s. In non-Olympic international competition, the Winnipegger won a gold medal in 1990 and gold and silver medals in 1992, all for different classes of competition. However, her specialty was the lightweight double sculls: she and her partner won gold in 1993, 1994, and 1995.

Olive Bend had one thing — and probably *only* one thing — in common with Madonna. Bend grew up in a sports-loving family in Poplar Point, Manitoba. When World War II took male athletes to Europe and the Pacific, women's baseball flourished, as documented in the film *A League of Their Own*, starring the aforementioned Material Girl. Many of those athletes were farmgirls and small-town women who had grown up playing ball at picnics and other social gatherings, often with men. Bend pitched four no-hitters during her wartime career with the Rockford (Illinois) Peaches in the All-American Girls' Professional League. (Obviously it wasn't all-American at all.) Bend, who became Olive Little through marriage, passed away in 1987.

The Old-Time Country Fair
The turn-of-the-century fairs were agricultural exhibitions that celebrated the modernization of the most important industry on the Prairies. New techniques and the latest machinery were put on display. Dairy farmers, ranchers, grain

farmers, and farmwives were invited to put the fruits of their labours to the test in rigorously judged competitions. The many transplanted easterners and foreigners who had arrived to cultivate the untamed prairie were hungry for tips and ideas. Despite all the noble sentiment, the midway was an unshakeable presence, a travelling menagerie of games, freaks, fortune-tellers, and, for a time, burlesque shows of varying degrees of lewdness.

The unwinnable midway games that have drained many a modern wallet had their precursors in those early fairs: grooved bowling alleys, loaded dice, weighted cans that couldn't be knocked over. Many of the same newspaper editors who carped in print about the decline in fairground morality were seen "researching" their articles. The number of fairs in the three Prairie provinces peaked in 1921 (108 in Alberta, 140 in Saskatchewan, and 70 in Manitoba). Drought and the Depression chipped away at those numbers: by 1935 there were only 72 country fairs held across the three provinces.

A Prairie newspaper long ago summarized the allure: "Perhaps the majority of people who attend exhibitions are more interested in frivolity than instruction, so that the impression which remains after an exhibition is over is often one flavored with the odor of the midway and the racing stable and the fireworks and the blah." "Blah" being the sound that one makes after three snow cones and a ride on the merry-go-round.

Flatland Festivals

Some citywide celebrations reflect the history and the nature of the host city. Edmonton has its Klondike Days, and the Stampede makes perfect sense for Calgary. But Prairie cities also host several music and arts festivals that attract top-notch international talent. The Edmonton and Winnipeg Folk Festivals are world-class. The Saskatoon Jazz Festival has brought the likes of Wynton Marsalis and his trumpet to the banks of the South Saskatchewan River. And each July campers arrive days early in the sleepy but scenic village of Craven, Saskatchewan, in anticipation of Rock 'N the Valley, a four-day celebration of rock music and alcohol poisoning. (Use the portable potties at your own peril — more than a few have been tipped over.)

Hundreds of small towns have one annual event, usually in late spring or summer, that may be little more than a crafts show, dinner, or modest midway. Souris, Manitoba, welcomes autumn with Scarecrow Days: all those hay-filled figures who stand motionless on the town's sidewalks really are a bunch of stuffed shirts. Besides providing a weekend of fun, these festivals give the locals something to work on together. That's the kind of bonding that turns a town into a community.

124

Sometimes these small places host big events. The National Ukrainian Festival takes place 10 kilometres south of Dauphin, Manitoba, in the first week of August. The many locals of Ukrainian descent put on a lively display of food, song, dance, and ceremony, including Obzhynky, their harvest festival.

In 1877 skating enthusiast Charles N. Bell skated the 29 kilometres from Winnipeg to Selkirk on the frozen Red River.

Local Passions

The residents of Macklin, Saskatchewan, have always engaged in the sport of Bunnock, also known as Bones. At first, it might look like a ghoulish version of horseshoes. Eight competitors divide into two teams and try to knock down the bones that their opponents have set on the ground. They do so by throwing bones of their own.

There are 52 bones: eight to throw ("schmeisers"), four guards, and 40 "soldiers." The guards and soldiers are divided equally, and then each team plants their guards and soldiers on the ground, 10 metres from where their opponents do the same thing. The teams take turns tossing their schmeisers, aiming for the guards first and then the soldiers.

Germans who emigrated to Russia's Volga region are credited with inventing the game. Their attempts to play horseshoes were thwarted: it was too hard to drive pegs into the frozen ground. The Germans realized that the ankle bone ("bunnock") of a horse could be set upright on the ground, just ready to be picked off. When they emigrated to Canada around the turn of the century, they brought the game with them, to Macklin.

In 1993 Macklin organized the first World Bunnock Championship Challenge. For one mid-August weekend, 400 players — many from Macklin and some from outside Saskatchewan and Canada — took up that challenge. An Edmonton squad came out on top. When competitors returned the following year, they were greeted by the world's largest bone, a 9.1-metre replica of an ankle bone at the entrance to the town.

Despite the event's growing popularity, no one is calling for random drug testing just yet — largely because no one knows which steroid you would take to become better at Bunnock.

For a brief period during the late 1880s, Lethbridge was the unlikely site of a fox-hunting craze. Townsfolk gathered to participate or just to watch. Anyone with a dog brought the animal along, whether it was a true blood-hound or not. On at least one occasion, the paper reported the sight of a fox running for its life through the streets of downtown Lethbridge, followed by a small parade of would-be captors.

Weirder still … Dugald is a town in Manitoba. A Wellington is a rubber boot. Each year, Dugald hosts the national Wellington-Boot-Throwing Championship. Contestants must fling a size-eight boot as far as they can. Points are awarded for distance, not style.

Canmore mountaineer Sharon Wood was the first North American woman to scale Mount Everest.

There are three reasons why the annual gopher races held in Eston, Saskatchewan, each July are better than horse races. (1) If a gopher breaks one of its legs, nobody gets really emotional when it's put down. (2) There is no need to train jockeys. (3) No one has ever had his or her thumbs broken over an unpaid gopher-race wager.

Shall We Dance?

Because no liquor was (officially) served, there were no liquor laws to govern the country dance and no closing time. People went home when the men got tired of swinging the women around and the women got tired of holding on for dear life. It wasn't uncommon for people to walk home guided by dawn's light.

The dances started a bit like a battle of the sexes. The men lined up along one side of the barn or hall, and the women took up positions along the far wall. When the music started, a man made a beeline for the woman whom he fancied. Many farm marriages wouldn't have happened without the dance.

The box social dance was a reversal of the modern bachelor auction. Women made lunches and took them to the dance in individually deco-rated boxes. The boxes were judged, but the big event was the auction: the successful male bidder won not only the boxed lunch but also the opportunity to sit down with its creator to eat it.

126

"They always bid the teacher's box up quite a bit," says a retired teacher who served eight years in rural schools. "If they knew the teacher was going with someone, the price got really high. He had to stay in the bidding if he expected that dance. If he didn't, she'd never let him forget it!"

The most enthusiastic dance fans were the Métis, who brought out the feet and the fiddles at every social gathering. A writer for an American magazine once described the frenzied, competitive nature of a Métis dance. Each couple tried to outperform the others with lively jigs and reels while the spectators roared and the fiddle sang "as if a devil was at a bow." One story tells of a Métis man who ran from Fort Garry to Headingly with a pedometer attached to him in order to settle an argument about the distance between the two communities. When he returned the next morning, the pedometer indicated that he'd covered 124 kilometres rather than the expected 32 kilometres. It turned out that there had been a dance at Headingly the previous evening.

I'm not sure why a recent nationwide study of per capita alcohol sales used a population group *aged 15 and over*. Perhaps it was the first Stats Can survey to take into account the existence of fake IDs. Anyway, it showed that in 1996 only New Brunswick saw lower per capita booze sales than Saskatchewan ($398) or Manitoba ($419). However, at $468, Alberta ranked fourth-highest among the provinces. This amount proves conclusively that oilmen and ranchers outdrink most farmers. Of course, the survey only measured liquor *sales*; there may still be a few stills brewing in the country homes of Manitoba and Saskatchewan.

The Stampede: Ready-to-Wear Heritage

Jeff Watson knows robotics. He doesn't know rodeo. He designs complex automated machinery. After all, he points out, that's why he gets paid the big bucks.

But put a black Stetson in Jeff's hands and his technosmarts mean little. Jeff surveys the felt headgear critically but admits that he doesn't really know much about the science of cowboy hats. He's considering the black hat, he says, because his T-shirt is black. "If I was wearing a brown shirt, I'd go for a brown hat."

"I thought I'd get a real cowboy hat to do some riding in the rain," he says, referring to the wet weather that's plagued Alberta all week. Then the Edmonton technophile confesses something that comes as less than a shock. "I'm a terrible rider."

But it's not just the riding. Jeff has come down to Calgary for the Stampede, like he does most years. "To see all the cowboys out to get killed," he says. And, on the grounds of the Calgary Stampede, home to the world's largest rodeo, even the most strong-willed robotics expert has a tough time resisting the urge to join the crowd and buy a big black Stetson.

The 1988 Winter Olympics at Calgary were the first to be tobacco-free.

His friend is buying a hat too. Her third one, in fact. Her technique is a little different from Jeff's. She surveys the brim, bends it between her hands, flips it over, and checks the manufacturer. When she's home, she competes in western-style riding competitions, so she wants to look good. "Home" for Toini Pettersson is Sweden. Whereas she can describe the relative merits of the major hat makers, Jeff has to ask her how to tell the front from the back. (Every city person asks this question at least once.) So Jeff, who was born in Peace River and has lived his whole life in Alberta, takes style and riding tips from a Swede.

"A hat makes you a cowboy," surmises Norm Suenm, operations manager for Lammle's western clothing, the same store that's set up the very busy tent where Jeff, Toini, and many other weekend cowhands are buying their Stampede duds. "You can wear jeans, you can wear a shirt, you can wear a pair of boots, and you won't stand out," Norm says. "You put a hat on, you're a cowboy."

Straw hats start at less than $20. Wool-felt Stetsons retail for up to $100, and the best fur-felt models can top $1,000. At the Stampede, everyone wants to be a cowboy. But these wannabes don't have to brand a cow or rope a calf to do it. They only have to buy a hat. What other lifestyle is so accommodating? And, for most people, the hat goes into the closet the day that Stampede shuts down and doesn't come out for 51 weeks.

This is the allure of the Calgary Stampede, says Don Dempson. This former easterner wasn't just bitten by the Stampede bug. It devoured him. As a former rep for Kodak, he visited Calgary in the mid-1980s to secure sponsorship at the Stampede. He soon realized that the Stampede ain't no 10-day rodeo. It's a year-long cycle of planning and work, culminating in 10 days of unmatched civic pride. No other Canadian event draws the same amount of volunteer support or generates so much citywide hysteria. The only other time that the city was this "up" was for the 1988 Winter Olympics.

128

Don no longer works for Kodak, but he lives in Calgary and takes time off from his job as a tourism consultant to soak up the Stampede every day, from sunrise to long past sunset. Some days, he cruises the grounds, looking for people whom he can simply help to enjoy the Stampede better. He's the ultrabooster.

"The Stampede isn't 10 days. It's an attitude. It's a lifestyle, a way of life for people who live in Alberta," Dempson says. It's Calgary's week to flex the unique cultural muscle that defines the city's past, even if it's based as much on mythology as history. The event's appeal extends far beyond the Rockies. "If you travel to Israel, there are usually Calgary Stampede posters in the airport," he says.

"There's a group of people in Calgary who don't want to promote the western life. They want to talk about computers and oil and gas and the new glass buildings," Dempson says. However, nearly half the vehicles that drive into the parkades of those office towers each morning are pickup trucks. "It's frowned upon to wear a tie and a jacket during Stampede. You have business all being done in a western atmosphere."

And it's that environment that puts people like Jeff under cowboy hats for at least a week each year. The reason is simple. It's fun to play at being a cowboy, at any age.

St. James was home to James McKay (1828-79), a 135-kilogram farmer who hunted and raised buffalo, governed as an MLA, and was widely recognized as Manitoba's strongest man.

Don wears a hat too, but he's no cowboy. "I'm allergic to horses," he says. "I was taken out of the Stampede one year in an ambulance."

The romantic and sanitized image of the cowboy is not some 20th-century invention or phenomenon unique to Calgary during Stampede week. Even 100 years ago, immigrant men were known to dress up in cowboy gear so that they could be photographed and then send the pictures home to their families.

Rodeo has its own Thrilla in Manilla. Call it Hurta in Alberta. It happened in Calgary in 1912 and is widely regarded as the single most exciting moment in the sport.

Tom Three Persons was only 24 when he became the only Canadian to qualify for the final round of the saddle-bronc-riding competition at the first Calgary Stampede. His draw was a bad one. In fact, it was the worst. He drew Cyclone, a horse that had thrown 129 would-be riders in the previous seven years.

Three Persons rode last. And best. The horse was unable to toss, buck, or shake its young rider. With the eight-second time limit still years away, the young Blood from Cardston, Alberta, simply held on until Cyclone stopped storming.

Three Persons won the event. He never repeated that feat, but his memorable ride in front of thousands of people made him a legend and guaranteed his induction into the Canadian Rodeo Historical Association's Hall of Fame in 1983. Three Persons died in 1949, a successful rancher, and was buried with the medal that he had won for his famous ride.

In Calgary, a world-class rodeo cowboy is a local hero, but the sport that made Pete Knight a champion also took his life. The Calgary cowboy held the world bronc-riding title longer than anyone else. He won it four times and was headed for his fifth win in 1937 when he was killed inside the rodeo arena.

Plain Poetry

"Come and see the cowboy poets! Come and see the coooowboy poets! You thought the midway was bad, wait 'til you see the cowboy poets! More fun than a corn dog in your brother's hand."

Bryn Thiessen is pullin' 'em in at the Calgary Stampede. People wander in past him and look for a chair on the floor of the livestock barn. Some have come in to escape from the hellacious rain. Others are likely intrigued by Bryn's appearance, which closely resembles that of the sidekick in a bad western: flat black hat, red kerchief tied 'round the neck, and a ball-peen nose perched above a moustache waxed to two wire-thin points.

But most have come for an earful of cowboy poetry, the increasingly popular genre that dresses up ranch life in rhyme, metre, and reflection. And, in Bryn's case, in humour.

On stage, introducing the other poets, Bryn comes off like a stand-up comic, tossing out rehearsed banter and off-the-cuff repartee with understated wit and colourful cadence. Of the half-dozen other performers this night, most have actually worked on a ranch. Bryn owns the Helmer Creek Ranch, a cattle and horse operation outside Sundre. "Given a chance, I would rather be known as a good hand than as a cowboy poet," he says.

"What we call cowboy poetry was an oral tradition. Most forms of poetry are like that worldwide. They're stories that can be remembered." The tradition goes back to cattlemen and cowboys who told stories and composed rhymes to entertain themselves and each other on the long, lonely cattle drives. Nobody called it cowboy poetry, even when a few published their poems. Growing up on an Alberta ranch, Bryn often made up little rhymes, but he was too shy to share them with anyone. In the mid-1980s, when Bryn was in his 20s, he got wind of the movement that was spreading up from annual gatherings of like-minded practitioners in the United States. In 1988 it spread to Pincher Creek, where western Canadian poets still gather for yearly festivals.

"A lot of it is humorous, because people like to laugh, but even people who are funny will say something that means a lot to them." Bryn proves this point minutes later by choking up midway through a reading of a melancholy song-poem about a cuckolded husband whose wife grants him one last dance before she walks out the door.

Balgonie's annual Bed Derby is clean fun between the sheets. Each year, teams of six race wheeled beds 18 kilometres from Regina to Balgonie.

"A lot of it deals with life, with facts, and with feelings," Bryn says. A cowboy poet will sing the praises of his horse as devoutly as Wordsworth rhapsodized about the English countryside. Of course, Wordsworth never had to think of a rhyme for "manure."

"JUST LIKE DAD"
This saddle that I'm riding
Was an old one of my dad's,
And this old hat I'm wearing
Is one that he once had.
I'll grow to be just like him,
For I never had a brother,
And if I grow this mustache thicker
Then it won't look like Mother's!
— Bryn Thiessen, *reprinted with permission*

Chapter 7

Our Arts
and Education

MABEL GEARY: "THE OTHER SIDE OF THE DESK"

"Alberta was getting fairly well-populated and making a lot of children,"
Mabel Geary remembers. "When they would get upwards of 10 or 20 children
in a community, they would look at getting a school."

But the school was just a building. The engine of learning across the
Prairies was fuelled by the teachers, most of them women who were barely
older than their oldest students. Mabel was one. "Someone said, 'If you're going
to be a nurse, you have to have two and a half years [of] training.' A teacher
took one year. So did a stenographer, but I wasn't interested in stenography."
Beyond these jobs, women's career options ran a bit thin.

So, in 1926, the girl from Edmonton took her grade 11 education to
Camrose Normal School for a year of teacher training. (Teacher colleges were

133

called normal schools. I'm not sure what that suggests about all those people who chose some other career.) "We were being trained, really, to manage a rural school. You had to know how to divide your time between the grades."

Mabel was 18 years old when she started teaching. "I remember thinking, 'Well, I'm going on the other side of the desk now.'" She got her first job in Franklin, near Cooking Lake, just east of Edmonton. She brought her own set of encyclopedias because the three parents who made up the school board hadn't seen fit to buy any supplies, including books. Her salary was $840 for a 10-month year. The first cheque from the school treasurer came up short. He had decided to withhold some of her money and give it to her at Christmas, just to prevent her from wasting it. This act typified the power imbalance in the teacher-trustee relationship. During the Depression, some of the women weren't paid at all, but they held on to their precious jobs and hoped that the money would eventually arrive.

"The first school was a good old-fashioned, one-room schoolhouse with three windows on each side … I had to sweep the floor. It was an extra $2 a week, or was it a month? In the winter, because I had to light the fire in the morning, it was $4."

The teacher had to satisfy the school board and pass muster during the school inspector's dreaded annual visit. There was one other test.

"One of the things everyone had to do in those days was to have a Christmas concert. If you were a good teacher and put on a good concert, you got asked back. If you didn't put on such a good show, well, then they didn't need you. It was the big event of the year."

At her second school, Mabel endeared herself to the area farmers by applying her geometry skills to agriculture. "I had a little formula for telling how many tons were in a bale. Quite a few farmers came to me and asked me to measure their hay."

When a single woman as young as 17 moved into a small town or rural setting, single young men took notice. A few would knock on the door.

"A girl would go out and teach, and in a year or two [she] was married. She became a farmer's wife. In those days, you resigned from the school, because you were a woman. It wasn't discrimination at all; it was to give someone else a job, because your husband would take care of you."

But Mabel, who never married, stayed in the game, moving between towns in central Alberta.

The kids were poor, of course, but they were well-behaved. Many arrived on horseback and tethered the animals to the hitching post outside the school.

134

Many of the boys left at grade 8, having received as much education as was deemed practical for someone expected to work on a farm for the rest of his life. Mabel remembers asking some girls why they were 14 years old and only in grade 7. "One of them said, 'Well, Miss Geary, we couldn't go to school in the winter, and we missed out.' It was too cold — they couldn't find clothes to put on."

Winnipegger Muriel Denison's book *Susannah: A Little Girl with the Mounties* was made into a movie starring Shirley Temple in 1939. (Diabetics should take extra insulin before viewing.)

Training at normal school left teachers unprepared for the student behavioural problems that nowadays merit educational specialists. "One day, one boy picked up a poker by the stove and came toward me and said, 'I'll kill you!'" Mabel recounts. "I said, 'Arthur, what's your trouble?' I never did find out. I said, 'Put it down,' and he did."

In 1930 Mabel took a job at Wimbledon, Alberta, just in time for the economic collapse that infected Canada and the world. Her first year there, she earned $1,000. "That June they said, 'If you take $100 less, we'd like to take you for another year.'" The next year, same story, same pay cut. And the next year. "Everybody else was doing it, and you were lucky to have a job."

Mabel eventually earned her grade 12 diploma and an education degree. After World War II, she moved to Leduc, just in time for the town's oil boom. She lived in Edmonton at the time and didn't own a car. "I commuted. That wasn't a done thing in those days. I went out in the morning on a train. Sometimes, you could get a train in the evening. Most of the time, I used my thumb." She eventually bought a car and taught a total of 25 years in Leduc before her retirement in 1972. Today, from her home on a quiet, tree-lined street in south-central Edmonton, she can look out her door and see the brick building that used to be the city's normal school.

Several times since her retirement, Mabel has ventured back into the classroom to tell students and teachers alike of her experiences in the one-room schoolhouse. She's seen endless changes since she started teaching 70 years ago. When asked which has been the most dramatic, she doesn't choose some educational advance. Rather, her answer reveals how much the school itself has evolved since those frontier days. "Children today sitting on the floor in their ordinary clothes! We would never sit on the floor, with all the dust we had. It wasn't good for your shoes. You certainly didn't sit on it."

The highly restrictive code of behaviour expected from early teachers is evident from the "rules of conduct" issued by the principal of one Manitoba school in 1880. "Men may take one evening each week for courting purposes, or two evenings if they go to church regularly," it read. Women fared worse. "Women teachers who marry or engage in other unseemly conduct will be dismissed." The edict also recommended that teachers read the Bible, save their money, and be prepared to explain any aberrant behaviour, such as drinking, smoking, playing pool, or *getting a shave in a barbershop*! The job was not without its rewards. The same notice assured teachers that, if they did their job "without fault" for five years, they would earn a raise of 25 cents a week.

The One-Room Schoolhouse

The young women who arrived by train, armed with no more than a year's worth of teacher training, had to oversee a learning environment that would make any modern teacher shudder. Foremost, they had to educate several grades at once. What would it be like to explain the alphabet to one child and grade 9 math to another? Student attendance was sporadic, dictated by the weather, illness, and farm duties.

The teacher's venue was the legendary one-room schoolhouse. There was usually a wood-burning stove to make the winter lessons bearable. If the school hadn't been built to allow the maximum amount of sunlight through the big side windows, then the students' eyesight suffered. The teacher often lived in a "teacherage" — a tiny abode next to the school.

And, if all this wasn't enough, she likely had to contend with numerous marriage proposals.

Was it foresight or just good luck? In early 2002, the Saskatoon Public Library booked an up-and-coming Montreal writer named Yann Martel to come on staff in 2003 as a writer-in-residence. A few months after he agreed to come Martel won the ultraprestigious Booker Prize for his novel, *The Life of Pi.*

According to the 2001 census, 20 percent of adults in Manitoba had obtained a bachelor's degree or higher level of education. In Saskatchewan, the

136

figure was 18 percent. More than 21 percent of Albertans have letters after their names. Of course, many of them got their education in Manitoba or Saskatchewan.

Some Great Minds

An Edmonton-born scholar wrote one of the most-quoted and probably most-misunderstood lines of the 20th century. The man was Marshall McLuhan. The line was "The medium is the message."

McLuhan (1911-80) was educated at the University of Manitoba and at Cambridge University in England, where he obtained a Ph.D. in literature. It was during his lengthy tenure as an English professor at the University of Toronto that McLuhan began to attract international attention for his thoughts on the ways that modern information is presented and understood. He compared traditional "hot" media such as print and radio, which provide more detailed information and thus require less involvement from the audience, with "cool" media such as television, which requires the viewer to rely more on his or her own perceptions to interpret what is presented. Thus, each medium dials up a different response from the audience, affecting how the information is perceived. "The medium is the message" was a snappy sentence, but it scarcely began to sum up the complexity of McLuhan's ideas. Even in his day, his writing was recognized as an exploration into uncharted intellectual waters. His many books on communications include two undisputed masterpieces of modern thought, *The Gutenberg Galaxy: The Making of Typographic Man* (which won a Governor General's Literary Award in 1962) and *Understanding Media*.

**The Canadian Country Music Hall of Fame is in Calgary,
but it used to be in Swift Current, Saskatchewan.**

Nellie McClung (1873-1951) was born in Chatsworth, Ontario, but raised in Souris Valley, Manitoba. McClung wrote 16 books in her life, including a bestselling debut novel. She also blossomed into an effective orator for women's rights, prohibition, and workplace reform. The McClungs moved to Alberta, where Nellie joined four other women in launching "the Persons Case" in 1928. The five women asked if the British North America Act's declaration that "qualified persons" could be invited to join the Senate included women. The Supreme Court of Canada answered that, no, it did not. The British Privy Council came back with a more enlightened reply the next year. Yep, "persons" included men *and* women. The first female senator was appointed the following year, but it wasn't McClung, who had already served five years in the Alberta legislature (1921-26). Just as Prairie folks do today, she retired to Victoria, where she wrote several autobiographical books detailing her days in the suffragette movement.

BLACK INK UNDER A BLUE SKY: PRAIRIE JOURNALISM

Long before *Frank* magazine earned a reputation as a nasty, funny deflator of Canada's most inflated balloons, Bob Edwards stuck his razor-sharp pen into the flanks of the country's rich and powerful. The vehicle that enabled him to do so each week was the *Calgary Eye-Opener*.

Edwards was born in Scotland in 1859 or 1864 — he treated his birth date with the same casual respect for accuracy that made his writing so much fun. He emigrated to Canada in 1895 and two years later started his first paper in Wetaskiwin, Alberta. He moved to High River, Alberta, which wasn't quite ready for his undisciplined style. He started the *Eye-Opener* there in 1902 but moved it to Calgary in 1904. It wasn't so much a newspaper as a distillation of his personality and perspective. Edwards found his targets in the halls of power and up and down Main Street. Calgary lawyer and future prime minister R. B. Bennett was first his nemesis and later one of his most loyal friends. Sometimes Edwards just made stuff up, as in his popular "Society Column."

Platinum-selling Celtic singer Loreena McKennitt grew up in the very nonmystical town of Morden, Manitoba.

His most famous invention was Peter McGonigle, a hard-drinking rogue with a résumé of illicit adventures. When Edwards described how none other than Lord Strathcona himself toasted the horse thief at a banquet, regular *Eye-Opener* readers knew to laugh along. A Toronto journalist less familiar with Edwards's "reporting style" rewrote the article and cabled it to a London daily. When Strathcona read the story over breakfast the next day, he initiated a series of angry telegrams and libel threats that took much diplomatic wrangling to put to rest.

138

The paper's circulation extended far beyond Calgary, and so did Edwards's influence: the paper's national circulation peaked at 35,000. The publication wasn't simply a laughing matter. The *Eye-Opener* added its weight to a host of controversial social and political issues, including women's suffrage, old-age pensions, and (if you can imagine) Senate reform. Back then, a journalist worried more about missing last call than about being sued. (Edwards was never successfully sued, and he rarely missed last call.) Anyone who knew about his fondness for drink was likely surprised by his protemperance stance on the eve of a prohibition plebiscite in 1915. He even sat as an independent member of the Alberta legislature from 1921 to 1922.

Defining good writing, Edwards advised: "Write in the fewest possible words and, when you have written it, stop and don't try to say it over again." Here is a selection of those "fewest possible words" that he employed so keenly:

- "There isn't a woman alive so bad in arithmetic that she can't calculate how much her husband would save if he didn't smoke."
- "Although the citizens of Calgary are not what you'd call violently insane, they still indulge in picnics to an alarming extent, eating sand and ants and doing other things which we admit are mildly idiotic."
- "A girl should never marry until she is fully competent to support a husband and then she shouldn't marry that kind of man."
- "John Moran of Sunnyside, who was killed last Wednesday by a Ford car, was a good fellow and deserved a more dignified death. There will be a sale of empty bottles at the Moran residence on Saturday afternoon at 2 o'clock to defray the funeral expenses."

Edwards died in 1922. He was buried in his casket with the last issue of the *Eye-Opener* and a flask of whisky — the ink and the drink. We don't know which he opened first.

Nicholas Flood Davin came to a bad end on October 18, 1901, alone in a Winnipeg hotel room with a hole in his head and his pistol by his side. His 58-year journey from birth in Ireland to that sad moment was far more triumphant. The founder of the Regina *Leader* and Saskatchewan's most important pioneer journalist was a dramatic and larger-than-life individual at a time and in a place that called for just that sort. Trained as a lawyer, he preferred to work as a journalist in England and then in Ontario. Davin moved west, and in 1883 he founded the *Leader*. Two years later, he engineered a scoop by disguising himself as a priest in order to interview Louis Riel in his cell.

Ever ambitious, he moved into politics and served as the Conservative MP for Assiniboia West from 1887 to 1900. When his career and finances declined, Davin took his own life.

Western Canada's first newspaper played a pivotal and in many ways unfortunate role in the development of Manitoba.

The *Nor'Wester* set up shop in 1859 in Assiniboine, right in the heart of Métis country. William Coldwell and William Buckingham, both British-born, brought their press up from St. Paul, Minnesota, by steamer, train, and oxcart. The *Nor'Wester* lobbied for a passing of ownership of the region from the Hudson's Bay Company to the British colony, ignoring the fact that the many French-speaking Métis might not have wanted to see their land under the rule of an English-speaking government.

That lack of understanding turned to outright contempt under the ownership of Dr. John Schultz, who bought the paper in 1864. The fiercely anti-Catholic Orangeman was never above distorting the facts and inflating hysteria in order to further his vision of a Métis-free settlement under the control of the Canadian government. Schultz sold the paper to the like-minded Dr. Walter Bown in 1868, and the continued pro-Canada, anti-Métis editorial position led to the paper's demise. When Louis Riel's provisional government was established in 1869, the *Nor'Wester* was suppressed. It was never published again. It was replaced as the region's paper by the *New Nation*, which rejected Canadian affiliation and instead suggested that the region would be better served as a slice of the American pie.

Bob Edwards may have been more colourful, but no figure in Prairie journalism was as respected as John W. Dafoe. It was under his tenure as editor that the *Manitoba Free Press* (renamed the *Winnipeg Free Press* in 1931) became recognized as the nation's best daily and one of the best newspapers in the world. That a paper outside the political and business epicentre of southern Ontario was held in such esteem made his stewardship all the more remarkable.

Dafoe, who looked a bit like James Joyce after a sleepless night, was 18 when he started in journalism as a rookie reporter at the *Montreal Star* in 1883. He was appointed editor of the *Manitoba Free Press* in 1901 and remained so until his death in 1944. He never backed down from any issue; he was one of the few Canadian newspapermen to openly denounce Britain's efforts to appease Hitler in 1938. Dafoe displayed unwavering nationalism that was inclusive.

Canada was for everyone, he maintained. However, the lifetime Liberal might have preferred a nation devoid of Tories and socialists alike.

The *Manitoba Free Press* started in 1872 with an unplanned advantage: angry mobs had destroyed the offices of three competing papers, enabling the new publication to snare a disproportionate share of the city's literate.

Prairie Pens

Some writers become forever associated with a particular place and time, an environment in which they lived and that they portrayed in print. No writer has been more strongly associated with what we call "Prairie life" than the recently departed W. O. Mitchell.

William Ormond Mitchell was born in Weyburn, Saskatchewan, but his portraits of childhood in *Who Has Seen the Wind* and the countless *Jake and the Kid* radio scripts depict an experience that thousands of Prairie people share. The experience may be common, but his gift for language, imagery, and humour was his own. *Who Has Seen the Wind*, published in 1947, was an instant hit and became a Canadian literary classic. His second novel, *The Kite*, wasn't published until 1962.

As a child, Mitchell moved with his mother to California and Florida. After leaving the University of Manitoba to spend the 1930s travelling and working abroad, he completed his education at the University of Alberta in the 1940s. He taught for two years, worked as fiction editor at *Maclean's* for three years, and spent most of this period in High River. In 1968 he moved to Calgary, where he remained until his death from prostate cancer in 1998.

Mitchell loved the theatre; he studied playwriting at the University of Washington in the 1930s and acted in Seattle from 1934 to 1936. His theatrical bent was obvious in his many public readings, where his rumpled appearance, warm manner, and colourful cadence made him a much-loved Canadian figure.

Mitchell was named to the Order of Canada in 1973 and was twice awarded the Stephen Leacock Medal for Humour. His greatest accomplishment was simply this: he wrote the Great Prairie Novel, one that entertains and enlightens as it preserves forever a place and a way of life.

As for Me and My House, a very different type of novel, might challenge *Who Has Seen the Wind* as the best depiction of Prairie life during the Depression. Born near Prince Albert, Saskatchewan, Sinclair Ross worked in a bank because his writing initially didn't sell well enough to pay the bills.

141

In fact, it was some years after the publication of *As for Me and My House* in 1941 that its artistry and importance were recognized. His first novel depicts the lonely, discouraging life of a minister and his wife, who have lived in a series of poor Prairie towns.

M anitoba's greatest novelist? Has to be Margaret Laurence, who patterned the fictional town of Manawaka on her hometown of Neepawa and then populated it with unforgettable characters such as Hagar Shipley, the stubborn and unforgiving heroine of *The Stone Angel*.

Born in 1926, Laurence attended Winnipeg's United College and, from 1949 to 1957, lived in Somalia and Ghana with her husband. That period fuelled five of her books. She lived intermittently in Canada and England after that. During this period, she wrote the five Manawaka novels, culminating in *The Diviners*, her last and, many believe, her best novel.

Laurence died in 1987. Her childhood residence at 312 First Avenue in Neepawa has been turned into a museum.

S ettlers of the Marsh, Manitoba schoolteacher Frederick Philip Grove's 1925 novel about a settler betrayed by sexuality, introduced realism to Canadian fiction. However, such realism was missing from his own account of his life. Grove claimed to be the child of wealthy Swedes who owned a castle. In fact, he was born Felix Paul Greve, the son of a poor German family, and was imprisoned in France for fraud before moving to Canada and assuming a new name. He wrote many novels, all of which pushed the envelope in their explorations of human relationships.

G abrielle Roy (1909-83) wasn't really a Manitoba writer. Her first and most famous book, *Bonheur d'occasion* (released in English as *The Tin Flute*), is a realistic depiction of lower-class Montreal, where she lived as an adult. However, she was born in St. Boniface and taught in rural schools in Manitoba before her first book was published. She did set a number of her books in the Prairies, including *Street of Riches* and *Where Nests the Water Hen*.

T he 1995 Pulitzer Prize for literature, one of the most prestigious literary awards in the world, went to then-Winnipeg author and University of Manitoba professor the late Carol Shields. *The Stone Diaries* also won the National Book Critics' Circle Award and a Governor General's Literary Award.

Guy Vanderhaeghe's 1996 novel *The Englishman's Boy* examines the Cypress Hills Massacre of 1873 and the early days of Hollywood filmmaking. It brought the Saskatoon writer his second Governor General's Literary Award. Vanderhaeghe, born in Esterhazy, Saskatchewan, won the same award in 1982 for his short story collection *Man Descending* — his first book!

The most famous poem by Calgary-born poet Earle Birney (1904-95) is "David," about a young man paralyzed by a fall during a rock-climbing adventure who begs his best friend to roll him off the ledge and end his suffering. Cheerful stuff. It appeared in Birney's first collection, *David and Other Poems*, which garnered him his first of two Governor General's Literary Awards.

Rudy Wiebe's novels have borrowed from history — Canada's and his own. The Edmonton author was born near Fairholme, in northern Saskatchewan, to German-speaking Mennonites who had emigrated to Canada at the start of the Depression. The experiences of and issues facing his people have been central in several of his works. Wiebe has also examined historical figures in *The Temptations of Big Bear* and *The Scorched-Wood People* (about Riel). He co-wrote the two-part miniseries *Big Bear*, based on *The Temptations of Big Bear* and broadcast on CBC TV in early January 1999.

Before Ontario-born Peter Gzowski became *Maclean's* youngest-ever managing editor and CBC Radio's best-known personality, he became the youngest-ever city editor of the *Moose Jaw Times-Herald* ... at age 20.

Although not of the stature of W. O. Mitchell, Max Braithwaite established himself as another tongue-in-cheek chronicler of Prairie adventures. *Why Shoot the Teacher?* is a comic remembrance of the one-room schoolhouse. The 1976 film version — starring *Harold and Maude*'s Bud Cort — was a hoot. Braithwaite's 25 books include *Never Sleep Three in a Bed* and *The Night We Stole the Mountie's Car*, which won the Stephen Leacock Medal for Humour in 1972. Braithwaite was born in Nokomis, Saskatchewan, in 1941 and died in 1995.

Many literary masterpieces were only possible because of the ways in which the authors were affected by their physical surroundings. Charles Dickens

143

couldn't have written *The Adventures of Huckleberry Finn*, and Margaret Atwood couldn't have penned *Who Has Seen the Wind*. Here's how Saskatchewan writer Brenda Riches described the impact of the prairie landscape on her and her peers:

"The Saskatchewan landscape has affected me profoundly. It has loosened something inside me so that I've discovered subjects to write about. And this loosening is somehow related to the spareness and spaciousness of prairie. It is a place that leaves room around objects. This drives you back inside your head. You're not distracted by details."
— *from* Voices and Visions, *by Doris Hillis*

Putting Our Story Down on Canvas

Even though the personnel changed, the Group of Seven's numeric name remained the same (you don't mess with a successful logo). When J. E. H. MacDonald died in 1932, the surviving members invited Lionel LeMoine FitzGerald, principal of the Winnipeg School of Art, to join them, making him the last artist to belong to this talented ensemble. FitzGerald, who was known to paint in knee-high snow and frigid temperatures, used soft colours and favoured simple subjects such as still lifes.

For a brief moment, Regina caught the attention of the art world. Ronald Bloore, Ted Godwin, Arthur McKay, Douglas Morton, and Kenneth Lochhead produced a series of abstract paintings unlike anything else being done north of the 49th parallel. In the 1950s, art instructors Lochhead and McKay organized the Emma Lake workshops for artists, an annual two-week workshop featuring guest instructors. In 1959 the attendance of American painter Barnett Newman inspired and enlightened the five men. Their work came together in 1961 in Regina and, later that year, as a show that toured Canada. New York critic Clement Greenberg buoyed their reputation with high praise. As a productive single unit, "the Regina Five" was short-lived. Despite the buzz, a major show in Los Angeles was greeted less than enthusiastically, and the men soon went on to successful solo careers.

In 1892, Mary Elizabeth Porritt sailed from England for Canada, all by herself. She wore a little green dress, and while Mary is long since gone, her garment survives. It's on display at the Costume Museum of Canada in Dugald, Manitoba, along with 35,000 other artifacts, some of them dating back 400 years. The museum grew out of a vintage fashion show put on by the Dugald Women's Institute in 1953. Among its many exhibits is an Elizabethan table napkin from 1565.

144

Crafting Our History

If you think that Prairie crafts begin and end with pictures of grain elevators painted on old saw blades, then you probably haven't been to one of our craft shows. We excel at a variety of homemade crafts, some of which are overt expressions of our heritage. This is quilt country; quilting clubs exist across the Prairies in small towns, cities, and on First Nations reserves (where the Native designs make for beautiful bedding). I've seen a young Saskatchewan woman use blown glass to replicate wheat. She once "planted" several thousand of the stems into a base and made a sparkling, tinkling glass wheat field.

The craft that is most clearly a product of our unique environment is wheat weaving, in which actual stalks of grain are tied together to make three-dimensional ornaments such as table settings or arranged artfully into detailed Prairie scenes suitable for framing.

The agrarian play *Paper Wheat* debuted in Saskatoon in 1977 and went on to Toronto.

The intricate, busy designs on Ukrainian Easter eggs are undeniably pretty, but they're also loaded with meaning. The art of *pysanky* has flourished as a visible element of Canadian-Ukrainian culture. The patterns painted on the eggs follow time-honoured motifs: animals, plants, and most often geometric designs. Each pattern is rich in symbolism. A hen represents fertility (not surprising given the medium). A tree represents strength or the Tree of Life. A deer denotes prosperity. The oft-used triangle stands for any trio, such as air, fire, and water. The lines that encircle the egg represent eternity. Even the colours are significant, reflecting everything from innocence or bravery to a bountiful harvest. The artist draws the pysanky — the designs — on the egg with a *kistka*, a tiny brass cone on the end of a stick. The cone is dipped in beeswax, and the colours are applied with special egg dyes, one at a time, with a layer of wax between each colour. When the dyes are dry, the wax is removed, and the egg is ready for a hard glossy coating. The pysanky are taken to church in a basket for blessing on Easter Sunday. A blessed pysanka is purported to possess talismanic powers. Although the eggs are closely associated with Easter, the form actually dates back to pre-Christian times, when they were used to worship the coming of spring.

A Weyburn restaurateur may have cornered the market on his particular hobby. Zia Yazdani was reportedly the only person in the world who painted Persian miniatures on eggs. In 1995 he saluted his favourite singer by painting Frank Sinatra's image on an ostrich egg.

Buffy Sainte-Marie was born Beverley Sainte-Marie.

Singing Our Song

One of Canada's biggest contributions to rock music spent five formative years in Winnipeg. Neil Young and his mother moved there from Ontario when he was 14. He formed his first band, the Jades, and then his second, the Squires. In 1964 he quit school and eventually found his way to California and a 40-year career as one of rock's most important voices, capable of matching lovely lyrics to head-busting displays of guitar power.

Few Canadian rock groups have ever achieved the popularity of Winnipeg's Chad Allen and the Expressions. Well, the group's popularity didn't come until after a name change to the Guess Who. Songs such as "These Eyes," "Undone," and the unneighbourly anthem "American Woman" made it Canada's biggest rock band in 1970, no contest. "American Woman" was the first Canadian song to reach top spot on the American hit parade. The boys performed it at the White House as a guest of President Richard Nixon. Like many people, Nixon probably thought that the spirited chorus was a celebration of women south of the border. In fact, the stanzas in between cited a litany of American problems.

Guitarist Randy Bachman left in 1970 to form the harder-sounding Bachman Turner Overdrive. Lead singer Burton Cummings went on to a successful solo career in the late 1970s and early 1980s. The other band members included Gary Peterson, Kurt Winter, Don McDougall, Jim Kale, and, during those first few years, Chad Allen. The Guess Who disbanded in 1975, but a successful reunion concert in the late 1990s convinced them to tour again.

Canadian pop acts still struggle to break into the U.S. market. The Guess Who was one of the first groups to succeed south of the border.

Joni Mitchell was born Roberta Joan Anderson in Fort Macleod and raised in Saskatoon. She wrote and sang introspective poetry that put her on top

146

of the crowded singer-songwriter scene of the early 1970s. Her fourth album, *Blue*, is a folk-rock masterpiece. Other singers scored with her songs first, notably Judy Collins with her rendition of "Both Sides Now," but Mitchell came into her own with hits such as "Big Yellow Taxi," "Carey," "This Flight Tonight," and "Help Me."

Mitchell hasn't retired, though she's slowed her pace, releasing an album every three years or so. In 1997 she made headlines as a musician (elected to the Rock & Roll Hall of Fame & Museum in Cleveland) and as a mother. She was reunited publicly — and happily — with the daughter whom she had given up for adoption in 1965.

Although Buffy Sainte-Marie has released many albums, she is known primarily for one song: "The Universal Soldier." The anti-war folk song brought her quick fame in 1963 at the age of 22. Sainte-Marie was born on the Piapot Reserve north of Regina but raised in Massachusetts by adoptive parents. She has never hidden her Cree background; rather, she has made it a part of her public persona.

Another strong and colourful Prairie singer has inspired so much controversy, much of it unintended, that many people have overlooked her tremendous talent. When k. d. lang first appeared in 1984 with a Grand Ole Opry fashion sense and a punk hairstyle, folks didn't know what to make of her. The product of tiny Consort, Alberta, applied her big, expressive voice and her love of Patsy Cline to a unique country-punk hybrid. The country music connection grew less explicit as her career progressed and disappeared completely when she made *Ingénue* in 1992, a lovely and emotional set of torch songs. By then, k. d., Kathy to her friends, was a worldwide star, turning up on the cover of *Vanity Fair* (dressed as a man and getting a shave from supermodel Cindy Crawford). She has won a Grammy for top female vocalist and was named to the Order of Canada in 1997. Her vegetarianism rankled some people in her cattle-country hometown. Likewise, her open lesbianism has left Nashville's traditionalists a bit unsure of what to make of her. It no longer matters: lang has long grown beyond worrying about how she or her work is perceived. She just *is*.

If it hadn't been for a broken leg suffered in a rodeo accident, Ian Tyson might have become a rodeo cowboy. The 19-year-old's aunt gave him a guitar to pluck while he recuperated, and his life took a fortunate detour. He took his country and rockabilly influences east, where he met folkie Sylvia Fricker. They became musical and marital partners, and Ian and Sylvia became stars of the North American folk scene of the early 1960s. They've since split up, and you don't hear Ian on the radio much anymore, but their song "Four Strong Winds" remains a Canadian classic and a common cover at the nation's folk festivals. Tyson was born in Victoria, but he's been closely associated with Alberta since he bought a cattle ranch in the foothills of the Rockies in 1980. He really is a singing cowboy.

From modest beginnings in 1974, the Winnipeg Folk Festival eventually became North America's largest such event and, some would attest, its best. For a three-day weekend each July, wooded Bird's Hill Park outside Winnipeg becomes Manitoba's third-largest city. Before performers and fans converge to partake in this massive, upbeat celebration of music, hundreds of volunteers do all the hard work necessary to pull it off. Organizers once received a letter from a fan in Bismarck, North Dakota, that tried to identify that special something: "A strong undercurrent of sanity binds the place together. People bring their babies and their grandmas and their banjos, making the gathering complete. The music doesn't shut anyone out by being too loud, raucous or obtuse. That's why folk music will live on, while the other muzaks will peter out."

Fame and Fortune

Vancouver likes to claim Michael J. Fox as its own because he went to school there, but he was born in Edmonton. The diminutive film and TV star is one of many people whom the Prairies have contributed to the entertainment industry and the arts world. Listing all of them would take an entire book, but here are some, with their hometowns:

- artist William Kurelek, whose paintings reflect his boyhood as the son of Ukrainian settlers in Whitford, Alberta
- Governor General's Literary Award recipient and poet Dorothy Livesay (Winnipeg)
- photographer Roloff Beny (Medicine Hat)
- bawdy folksinger Oscar Brand (Winnipeg)
- playwright George Ryga (Deep Creek, Alberta), author of *The Ecstasy of Rita Joe*
- Robert Goulet, born in the United States but raised in Edmonton and Toronto on his way to becoming one of the more bankable stars of musical theatre and film during the 1960s and 1970s

148

- Arthur Hiller (Edmonton), who worked for CBC TV before moving to Hollywood to direct films, including *Love Story*, the top-grossing film of 1970
- stage and screen actress Frances Hyland (Shaunavon, Saskatchewan)
- Winnipeg's Crash Test Dummies, who appeared on *Saturday Night Live* and saw their second album succeed wildly in the all-important U.S. market
- multi-platinum rock band Nickelback (Hanna, Alberta)
- Allen Sapp, whose ability to recall precise moments from his upbringing on the Red Pheasant Reserve in Saskatchewan has made him one of Canada's most decorated artists
- the Stampeders (formed in Calgary, of course), whose song "Sweet City Woman" was a huge radio hit in 1970.

What's in a name? For Regina's Dick Assman, 15 minutes of fame and an appearance on David Letterman's *Late Show*. Someone sent Letterman a newspaper ad for Assman's gas station, and the late-night talk show host turned the gas jockey's surname into a running gag for several weeks in 1995. "Assmania" swept Canada. In the Queen City, people lined up in their cars to have their gas pumped by the overnight celeb. Letterman flew Dick down for a quick appearance, but it took about a year for the craze to subside.

Fay Wray's star rose high — to the top of the Empire State Building, in fact. Wray was born in Cardston, Alberta, where her father ran the sawmill. She was still a girl when her family moved to Arizona and then to California, where she became an extra in silent films. Her big break came in 1933, when she was cast as one player in a very unconventional and scary love triangle called *King Kong*. Wray was so beautiful that a giant monkey believed that a mixed marriage could work. The romance fizzled — different backgrounds, conflicting career aspirations, in-law problems — but it was memorable. And boy could Wray scream! Her other films paled in comparison, and her star dimmed, although it was nice to see Billy Crystal introduce her during the 1998 Oscar telecast.

Wray may have been a one-hit wonder, but that one portrayal has guaranteed her cinematic immortality. She will exist forever in one of Hollywood's most unforgettable images, even if it's one that she shares with five huge, hairy fingers.

Former brat-pack actor Kiefer Sutherland is the grandson of Tommy Douglas. The late Saskatchewan premier's daughter, Shirley Douglas, married esteemed Canadian actor Donald Sutherland. Kiefer has thought about making a film about his grandfather.

149

Who could have guessed what was going on behind Leslie Nielsen's stern facade? Nielsen appeared in movies such as *Forbidden Planet* and *Tammy and the Bachelor* and in many a 1970s crime drama, usually as some solemn hero, villain, or supporting player. His arched-eyebrow portrayals epitomized "straight" acting. In 1980 Nielsen got what turned out to be his big break in *Airplane!* — parodying roles that he had been playing for years. As the doctor who tries to calm his fellow passengers aboard the crippled plane, Nielsen delivers one straight-faced non sequitur after another, stiffer than Jack Webb and twice as funny. An example:

Nielsen: "We have to get to a hospital."

Other character: "A hospital! What is it?"

Nielsen: "It's a large building with patients, but that's not important now."

Nielsen employed the same comedic style in his portrayal of Lieutenant Frank Drebin in the TV series *Police Squad*. The show didn't last long — it was ahead of its time — but it did inspire several hit film versions. Nielsen hasn't looked back.

Most people already know all this about him. Few know that he was born in Regina. His father, a Mountie, was posted to Fort Norman, Northwest Territories, when Nielsen was still an infant. Five years later, the family moved to Edmonton.

The actor who once seemed straighter than straight simply bent that image until it broke. There's neither pun too awful nor pratfall too undignified for this very funny man.

The first university on the Prairies was the University of Manitoba, founded in 1877.

Michael Keaton as Batman. Tom Cruise as the vampire Lestat. Such infamous miscasting choices pale compared with that of the 1954 Universal Studios movie *Saskatchewan*. Alan Ladd foiled the Indians — and trampled Canadian history — when he broke up Sitting Bull's plan to take over western Canada. And if something about Saskatchewan didn't look quite right, then that's because the exteriors were shot in the Canadian Rockies.

150

Long before Toronto started its international film festival, a tiny city in southeastern Saskatchewan began hosting such a festival. Since 1950 world-famous directors, ingénues, topless beach bunnies, and paparazzi have all completely ignored the Yorkton festival for short-subject films and videos. However, you might meet many aspiring filmmakers nominated for a Golden Sheaf Award, a few TV deal makers, and plenty of locals who come out for the downtown street dance held in conjunction with the festival.

Under the Lights

Shadow of the Prairie by Gweneth Lloyd was one of many ballets written for the Royal Winnipeg Ballet. The country's oldest continuing ballet — and undoubtedly our most famous — was founded by Lloyd and Betty Farrally in 1938 as part of their ballet school. It became fully professional 11 years later. However, it took two performances — in 1951 and 1953 — in front of Elizabeth Windsor, who became Queen Elizabeth II on February 8, 1952, before it was granted the right to use the word *royal* in its title.

The company was forced into a two-year hiatus when a fire destroyed all its property in 1954. The company formed its own school in 1962 and has nurtured an international reputation for wedding classical form to contemporary ballet. In 1966 it staged the first full-length ballet by a Canadian. One of the best things about the RWB is that it dispels the notion that a Prairie cultural event has to have hay on the floor.

In late-19th-century Winnipeg, the lack of real theatres led to some necessary compromises. For a time, plays were staged in the loft above a feed store; the proprietor, a Mr. Lyons, had to put up a notice: "The audience is requested not to applaud for fear the building will collapse."

The first Canada Council grant to study magic was awarded to Doug Henning in 1970. He was born in Fort Garry, Manitoba, and went on to become one of the world's best-known magicians. He was able to convince people of all manner of illusions, except when he announced that the carpet-riding, levitating Natural Law Party was the one to support in the 1993 federal election. His audience finally refused to suspend disbelief.

Brad Fraser was only 20 when his first play was staged at a professional theatre. The board of Edmonton's Walterdale Playhouse decided that the tale about institutionalized teenagers was too sexual and vulgar and nearly cancelled it days before the premiere. It didn't, though, and *Mutants* became a hit. *Unidentified Human Remains and the True Nature of Love* and *Poor Super Man* in the 1990s established Fraser's international reputation. The openly gay Edmontonian attracted attention for his sexually adventurous plot lines and caustic dialogue. He moved to Toronto and, for a while, he was writing film scripts ... for Disney!

The most important trial on the Prairies — sorry, Colin Thatcher — started on July 20, 1885, in a packed Regina courtroom. It ended on August 1 with a verdict of guilty — Louis Riel was officially branded a Canadian traitor.

Every summer since 1967, Jesse Coulter's *The Trial of Louis Riel* (commissioned to celebrate the nation's centennial) has been performed for Regina audiences as well as visitors from down the road and across the ocean. The script is a dramatic re-creation that offers an edited, two-hour transcript of original testimony. For years it was the second-longest continually running play in North America. (Prince Edward Island's *Anne of Green Gables* was first.) In 2003, the producers announced the curtain would finally come down on the 36-year-old play.

Each night, the players invited six men from the audience to come onstage and play the jury, giving them an onstage view of the proceedings. For the play's finale, the men were escorted offstage to the unseen jury room to deliberate. The other characters conferred, and Riel pondered his fate for two minutes of condensed time, after which the jurors filed back in with the final word. Del Fraser, who played Riel in nearly 400 performances since 1977, remembers a performance in which he found himself waiting an awfully long time for the jury to return. He clasped his hands, looked heavenward, stared at his feet, and performed every other "waiting" action short of reading a magazine. After an agonizing few moments for all the bewildered actors, the jury returned and delivered the expected verdict. After the performance, Fraser learned what had caused the delay. "The man playing the foreman had said 'This guy's not guilty!' " It had taken several minutes of backstage lobbying by the other jurors to convince the foreman to stand up and read the "proper" verdict.

Some Artsy Connections

Our very own Margaret Laurence has a connection to Paul Newman. It's one of several links between the Prairies and internationally known figures.

Newman directed his wife, Joanne Woodward, in *Rachel, Rachel* in 1968. The movie, about a lonely spinster teaching school in rural Connecticut, is based on Laurence's 1966 novel *A Jest of God.*

Winnipeg-born singer Terry Jacks enjoyed two astronomical (albeit schlocky) pop hits: "Which Way You Goin', Billy?" with the Poppy Family, and "Seasons in the Sun" as a solo artist.

One of the best-known creations in children's literature might be known by some wildly different name today if it hadn't been for a Winnipeg vet.

One summer day in 1914, Harry Colebourn was travelling by train from Winnipeg to Quebec, along with other members of the Second Canadian Infantry Brigade. The war in Europe beckoned. While passing through a northern Ontario town, Colebourn paid a trapper $20 for a black bear cub. Colebourn named her Winnipeg, but soon all the soldiers were calling their new mascot Winnie.

The brigade — including its newest recruit — travelled onward to England. When Colebourn's turn to fight came, he entrusted the bear to the London Zoo. Oddly this wasn't that strange a practice. Four of the zoo's other bears during this period were left there by Canadian soldiers. At war's end, Colebourn donated the bear to the zoo permanently.

Winnie was a show business natural. Friendlier and funnier than the others, she entertained thousands of British children until her death in 1934. One of them was Christopher Robin Milne, who attended the zoo with his father, author Alan Alexander Milne. When a London newspaper commissioned the elder Milne to write a Christmas story in 1925, he created a teddy bear named Edward. The following year, the bear had a new name, Winnie the Pooh, and starred in the first of a bestselling series of books.

What does a small Saskatchewan town near the Manitoba border have to do with Russia's greatest author?

The Doukhobors, a religious sect, left Russia in 1898 to escape persecution. They found a new home in eastern Saskatchewan and created a community that they named after their leader, Peter Veregin. A miniature village of re-created buildings shows visitors to Veregin how those first settlers lived.

There's also a statue of the man who rallied financial support to help the families make the move: *War and Peace* author Leo Tolstoy.

The great screen villain of 1968 wasn't a person at all. It was HAL 9000, the onboard computer that tries to rid the spaceship of its human occupants in *2001: A Space Odyssey*. HAL was never much more than a few blinking lights, but it was very much a presence in the film due to that calm and soothing voice, with a hint of off-kilter malevolence lurking underneath. It belonged to Douglas Rain, a Winnipeg-born stage actor.

Chapter 8

What We Believe

MORRIS ELFENBAUM: A PRAIRIE POSTER CHILD?

When you think of the Prairies, certain themes spring to mind. Agriculture, of course, and the rural lifestyle that has accompanied it. A political populism that was Aberhart's Social Credit for some folks and Douglas's CCF for others. Then there's religion, with its historical links to the various ethnic groups that moved here 100 years ago. And it wouldn't take long before the CFL would appear on that list.

Which makes Morris Elfenbaum something of a Prairie poster child. Mind you, it would have to be a pretty big poster. Morris stands six foot three and weighs 314 pounds. His 26-inch neck merges seamlessly with the silhouette of his great, balding skull. His chest is 61 inches around. His T-shirt is bigger than my apartment.

Morris entered this world a very normal six pounds and two ounces. That was the last time he was ever small. "When I started grade 1, I was heavier than the teacher," he says with customary good humour. Growing up an only child on a farm and ranch operation near Lipton, Saskatchewan, Morris was a godsend to his father. He grew up tossing hay bales as if they were dice.

Out of place on the playground and with no siblings, Morris often had to make his own fun. He fashioned a golf club out of a cane and would putt balls into gopher holes. "I had a ready-made golf course." Most farmers would love to have only 18 gopher holes on their property.

Morris took up several sports, including six-man football (a necessarily truncated form of the game found in some rural schools). He was surprisingly fast for his size, which neared 300 pounds by grade 12. It led to a scholarship to Minot State University in North Dakota. "They wanted the foot speed. They thought they could teach me the rest."

They did. The young offensive tackle was the first pick in the eighth round of the 1985 CFL draft. "I wanted to play in Saskatchewan. It was home and close to the farm." But Morris was picked by the other Roughriders — those in Ottawa. He had never forgiven them for beating Saskatchewan in the 1976 Grey Cup, and he didn't find much reason to change his opinion once he started salary negotiations with his new employers. "For what I could make playing in the CFL and what I could make farming at the time, it didn't make sense to play football."

So he never did. Not even one down. Instead, he farmed, took care of his mother, and dabbled in provincial politics, running unsuccessfully for the NDP nomination in Melville. The NDP's sweeping hospital closures in rural Saskatchewan soured him on the party and on politics. But only temporarily. By 2000, he was running for MLA in North Regina for the right-of-centre Saskatchewan Party.

In 1995 the Jewish-born Elfenbaum became a born-again Christian. He entered bible college and in 1998 graduated with a bachelor of religious education degree. Although he's pretty much guaranteed a job in the afterlife — Saint Peter could probably use a bouncer — Morris believes that this new field may one day take him outside Saskatchewan.

That prospect has him thinking of what he'll miss the most. "I'll miss some of the freedom the Prairies offer you. Like the ability to drive 15 minutes from Regina and go for a walk in the country." And the barn dances, he says. He remembers those nights. Right up to the early 1980s, it seemed, you could still find a local dance on a Saturday night. "Your neighbours all came, and there was a midnight buffet." A few towns still organize them, he points out, though not often.

"And no one uses barns anymore … I really miss them. It's one less thing to hold a community together," Morris says.

"The best thing was [that] you could count on your neighbours. I remember when our bunkhouse for the hired men burned when I was 13. Mom made one phone call, and in 20 minutes we had 70 people there, helping put it out. They couldn't save the bunkhouse, but they saved other buildings. They piled snow on the other buildings to prevent them from catching fire.

"I'll never forget stuff like that. People were always there."

Prairie people generally have a few things to say about the prairie and their relationships with it. Their thoughts below, some expressed directly to me and some unearthed from other sources, reveal more about the people who live beneath the big sky than statistics or studies ever could.

The People

"I've seen what happens to peas that are thawed and frozen and thawed and refrozen, and that's kind of how we are … we're freezing and we stick together in clumps."
— *Connie Kaldor, Saskatchewan-born singer-songwriter*

"Speaking personally, I was taken aback when a couple noticed my Quebec licence plates and said: 'Welcome to Regina.' A local garage owner inflated my flat tire without charge; my realtor helped me to adjust my windows and heating unit in my new home; the Sears appliance salesman offered to personally adjust my appliances' hoses and outlets for me."
— *Lenora Martin, new arrival from Montreal, 1998, editorializing in the* Regina Free Press

"Life is just a little bit harder here, and it makes people, well, when there's something to smile about, they smile. They really say 'Hello!' to you. They don't walk around with their heads down."
— *Lorraine Freeman, executive director of the Manitoba Métis Resource Centre*

The Hospitality

"Hospitality is most truly understood in the north-west of Canada. No guest ever seems to be found *de trop*. Householders leave the outside door unlocked at night, so that a wayfarer may be able to shelter himself till morning; and a sudden storm coming on, perhaps on Sunday evening, will add seven or eight people to the ordinary number on an outlying farm."

— *Catherine Johnstone (1838-1923), travel writer*

The Land

Jean Bates was born in Landscape, Saskatchewan. Big-L Landscape isn't much more now than a few buildings where memories outnumber inhabitants. Small-l landscape, at least, is still in abundance. And that's what Jean appreciates most about the Prairies.

"When I was a girl, I spent summer holidays at my grandfather's farm. They had a great big dugout full of water. You could go swimming in it. That was what we looked forward to every summer.

"A doctor married my sister. He came from Pembroke, Ontario, and he was just fascinated by our skies. They were so beautiful, he used to say, and we just took that for granted. I guess we do, too. As you get older, you learn to respect this and enjoy just sitting outside and watching ... My husband used to go hunting, and he would say how beautiful it was to sit there in the morning, watching the sun rise, just waiting for the poor ducks."

"I am really not chauvinistic about most things, but I think that the land that you walked over as a kid is in your blood like a salmon. I love the prairies. The prairie is like the desert down here (in California). Its beauty is subtler."

— *Joni Mitchell, 1987*

"The unending vision of sky and grass, the dim, distant and evershifting horizon, the ridges that seem to be rolled upon one another in motionless torpor; the effect of sunrise and sunset, of night narrowing the vision to nothing, and morning only expanding it to a shapeless blank; the sigh and sough of a breeze that sees an echo in unison with the solitude of which it is the sole voice; and, above all, the sense of lonely, unending distance which comes to the voyageur

when day after day has gone by, night has closed, and morning dawned upon his onward progress under the same ever-moving horizon of grass and sky."
— *Sir William Francis Butler, military officer and author, 1869*

"The first time I ever felt the necessity or inevitableness of verse was in the desire to reproduce the peculiar quality of feeling which is induced by the flat spaces and wide horizons of the virgin prairie of Western Canada."
— *T. E. Hulme, British critic, 1906*

"Our land is more valuable than your money. It will last forever. It will not perish as long as the sun shines and the water flows, and through all the years it will give life to men and beasts. It was put there by the Great Spirit and we cannot sell it because it does not belong to us."
— *Crowfoot, 19th-century Blackfoot chief*

Down on the Farm

"Farming was my best life in the world. Freedom and everything else. I like the outside air, and I think it's good for you." So says Adam Becker. He hasn't farmed since 1963, when he sold the wheat and feed operation that he got from his father near Schuler in southeast Alberta and moved to Medicine Hat.

Memory's kind perspective hasn't filtered out the tough times that dictated Adam's days as a farmer. "In 1937 the drought was terrible. We didn't get no crop at all." Adam is sitting on a simple kitchen chair in the hall of his small suite. Sunlight breaches the window and falls across his broad, lined features, illuminating him against the bare white wall. "It was really hard. There were some people, they had to save for their next loaf of bread. We had chickens, and they laid eggs, and we sold them to the store for five cents a dozen."

The Depression didn't pick and choose. Everyone was poor. Everyone understood. Notes Adam:

"They cooperated in all ways. I don't think we cooperate quite so good no more. When somebody built a building, neighbours all came together to help build it. There was no money involved … We were neighbours. We'd go 15, 20 miles sometimes, just to have a talk with them."

The hard times have never quite disappeared. Or, at least, they've always returned. Adam's son left the farm for a high-tech computing job in Medicine Hat only to be laid off after 16 years. Adam's wife died in the summer of 1998, three months shy of their 59th anniversary. She died of Alzheimer's, which Adam innocently refers to as "Oldtimer's."

He met her in a way that was fairly common for farm folks "back then." He went shopping. "We all had to go to town to buy a little groceries, and that's when you met people. And we'd talk. I'm a good talker."

Farmwives

"They didn't have the opportunity to go out and confront the land and the weather directly and make their peace with it the way men did; instead they sat inside and got sad. They lived and worked in a very small, constrained space, with the wind everlasting and whistling around the eaves. We talk about the men who tore up the prairie soil, but the people who suffered for that soil were the women."

— *Ralph Hedlin, Calgary writer and consultant*

Small-Town Life

"I can probably walk through town and get $150 worth of goods, and if I'm a little short that's okay. I can fill my truck up with gas, no cash. I can go to the grocery store, no cash. Everybody knows me. I'm not going anywhere ... They'll do anything for you at any time. No question. It's not even an issue. It's comforting."

— *Tom Heapy, Oak River, Manitoba*

"They (my two daughters) would walk with a wagon down to the store, and they'd come back with your groceries and a piece of candy. There's nowhere else on this planet that you can send three-year-old children to do your shopping for you."

— *Shaunavon, Saskatchewan, doctor Martin Vogel,*
  one of many South African physicians who have moved to rural
  Prairie towns

160

"Roads are everything in rural Saskatchewan. That's where most of our time is spent and to see our roads crumbling is a concern to us because it has a negative impact on all of rural Saskatchewan."
— *Sinclair Harrison, former president of the Saskatchewan Association of Rural Municipalities*

Tough Times ...

"In the 1930s, there was a camaraderie of suffering, no finger-pointing or assessing of blame. But today the greatest critics of farmers in trouble are farmers ... What's happened is if one points at another and says they are to blame because of their own mismanagement or greed, then you set yourself apart. But in the 1930s, there wasn't this stage-by-stage progression of people losing their farms. It was everyone together."
— *former Saskatchewan Liberal leader Lynda Haverstock, 1989*

... Surviving Them

"We had to depend on ourselves and on our near neighbours during that period, and I think it was good for us, even though it took a long time for that decade to pass. I think they call it character-building and it did no one any great harm. I know it produced a hardy, resilient breed of men and women you scarcely find anywhere else."
— *Roy Vanstone, Lang, Saskatchewan, 1984*

Better Times

"You could walk out of high school and get a job in an hour."
— *Calgary teacher Kathryn Richmond, on the 1970s*

What Is It about Cowboys?

"I think their strength and their character. Their ruggedness. Cowboys are more an institution, and they've got that quality about them. I'm not going to say wrangler butt!"
— *Kate McWhir, 1992 Calgary Stampede Princess*

"Cowboys are the real athletes. They get a broken arm, they still compete. You get hockey players with a hangnail who say, 'I can't compete.'"

— Frank Sisson, *Calgary casino owner and rodeo volunteer*

"There's a certain attitude, a certain work ethic. More than anything, it's an attitude of prioritizing what's really important. It's family, good friends, and a good work ethic. And great bucking horses!"

— Robin Burwash, *Canada's four-time top rodeo cowboy*

Yee-haaa!

"I'm not sure what a redneck is. Is Alberta redneck? I don't know. It's a myth that perpetuates. What's an Albertan anyway? There's a whole lot of non-Albertans living in Calgary ... Loud and boisterous? I don't know. I leave that to the Americans."

— Gordon Pittman, *Airdre businessman*

"What with murder trials, suicides, amputated legs, bear hunts, stray dogs, conventions, politics and other matters of interest too numerous to mention, our town is stepping quickly into the limelight of notoriety and no one can find fault at the dullness of life just now anyway."

— Red Deer News, *August 29, 1905*

"Moose Jaw was an anomaly in Saskatchewan ... an industrial town in an agricultural setting. In its early years it was a 'red light' city, and later, a union hotbed, long before there was union strength anywhere else in Saskatchewan. So to grow up in Moose Jaw was to live with a lot of contradictions. Maybe that's justifying the irrationalism of the place."

— Ken Mitchell, *writer and academic*

"I've lived here in the foothills under the jumble of the Rockies long enough to become infected with the Alberta strain of snobbery: horse snobbery. A year ago I did something about it and got rid of our four horses. To be among the select in Alberta one should be a descendant of a fine old ranching family. Failing that, simply be horsey; wear tulip-stitched, high-heeled, eighty-dollar riding boots, a white stetson and a string tie."

— W. O. Mitchell, *writing in Maclean's, May 16, 1964*

"Regina fans really made the difference. The town was dead until they arrived. The Grey Cup atmosphere took a long time coming. But by game time, everybody was rocking."

— *Calgarian Berne Chrisp at the 1989 Grey Cup game in Toronto*

"Around 1976 there was a movement to move away from the western image. It was an insecurity based on what we thought people from Toronto might think. Since the Olympics (in 1988) and what I would call a coming of age for Calgary, it gave us a whole renewed sense of pride. People are quite prepared to say, 'This is our history, and we're going to wear it with pride.' ... We had every reason to crawl into our shell in '82 when the oil price fell. We didn't. We kept struggling. We kept working on it. We decided to hold the best Winter Olympics ever. We did, and we ended up with a $150 million surplus ... There's a lot of successful people here who lost their jobs in '82."

— *former Calgary mayor Al Duerr*

The Rivalry

Andrew Yskes was born and raised in Calgary, moved to Toronto in the go-go '80s, and now lives with his family in Edmonton. He's worked in film and public relations and talks about Alberta's two major cities, including that endless rivalry.

"Calgary is exploding right now. 'Booming' is not a good word. It's exploding! It's losing a little bit of the friendliness. Edmonton hasn't really felt the impact of growth like Calgary does. In Edmonton, we feel slighted by businesses that pick Calgary over Edmonton for a head office when they move, for no reason other than it's closer to the mountains ... In Toronto, people were so busy. They kept to themselves. Now Calgary's getting like that. It affects people. They get a little more frustrated driving.

"Calgary is wonderful for its proximity to the mountains ... Edmonton has an incredible green belt. We have a river valley that is the envy of Calgary ... The rivalry is always there. It amazes me. It's really sports-based. 'Oilers suck. Flames rule.' 'All Calgarians are rednecks.' And 'Edmontonians are bureaucrats.' You listen to most people insult Calgary, and they have relatives there! And vice versa."

Andrew maintains that you can tell a native Calgarian by how he or she pronounces the city's name. Outsiders enunciate every syllable, with a slight

163

emphasis on the middle one: cal-GAR-ee. The native Calgarian reduces it to a two-syllable word and emphasizes the first one, perhaps to catch everyone's attention, like a cowboy kicking open the swinging doors of a saloon: CAL-gree!

Canada

"And when they [CBC] paid any attention to the West, there was always a mouth organ wailing, breezes blowing through the wheat and the picture of a rustic farmer. We're always portrayed as some sort of backwoods people."

— *I. H. Asper, Manitoba Liberal leader, 1973*

"If what is produced in Ontario is sold at higher than world prices in Western Canada, then I think that what is produced in Western Canada, ... natural gas, is not going to be sold at low world prices to the consumers in Ontario. You can't have it both ways."

— *James Richardson, western MP, 1973*

"We've accepted the fact that we couldn't be New York or Toronto ... We discovered the act of trying to be like them might destroy us. And so we've turned inward toward the search and discovery of what we are rather than what we are not."

— *Saskatchewan writer Sharon Butala in the* Globe and Mail, *1995*

Prairie Peculiarities, a.k.a. "Culture"

"During the broadcast of the game Saturday, Edmonton's streets were strangely silent and almost deserted. It was almost as if an air raid alarm had sounded, warning the citizens to take cover. Business almost came to a standstill as practically everyone huddled over radios in stores, offices and homes."

— *the* Toronto Star, *November 29, 1954, Grey Cup day*

"[Have] you read *Why Shoot the Teacher?* It was a lot like that. Families brought the babies to the school and put their babies on the teacher's desk, or else on the benches … Barn dances went on pretty nearly all night. I went with a gang — the kids I taught — and we'd go to a barn dance. We'd get home at about four in the morning, and everyone played ball until school started. We had a lot of energy in those days!"
    — *a former Alberta teacher*

"Strathcona is Edmonton's hip area. This is where all the trends start and finish … Edmonton is a comfortable city to live in, but it's certainly lacking in glamour … 'Hip' is a pretty general term. You can find it here. Skateboards are cool in Montreal, sure, and they're cool here. You like rap music? We've got that too. The rodeo is kind of uncool. There's nothing cool about chasing another creature hard into the ground."
    — *20-something store clerk Steve Tsongas*

"Being cut off from culture, so many people grow up with the redneck ideas. But you can find culture in the small places, you just have to look for it. In Lethbridge, they have an amazing gallery called the South Alberta Art Gallery. That's the cultural centre of Lethbridge … When I grew up [in Grande Prairie], everyone wanted to move to Vancouver and Edmonton. That feeling of isolation is very suffocating. You think if you get to a big city you'll be able to take that big gulp of air and feel the freedom. I like people who are into change and into culture, but you don't have to leave to get that … Prairie people have a kind of calmness or easygoingness compared to more cosmopolitan places. I think we are less rushed. A lot of the people are raised in farming communities, and they have that love of nature, and I think people from larger cities can't do that. How can they do that if they hang around downtown with trees that were planted in the cement?"
    — *former University of Lethbridge student Christina Kaulbach-Stosuy*

You Never Really Leave

"Switzerland has to be one of the most beautiful countries in the world, a picture postcard wherever you go. When I open the curtains in my apartment, I see the Alps. But you know, I do miss seeing the sunrises and the sunsets. You won't find the hospitality and friendliness that you find here anywhere else."

— *Regina-born software engineer Darryl Gebert,*
now living in Zurich

A Window on the 20th Century

Norman Chapman remembers a used clock lying amid the clutter of a secondhand store in small-town Manitoba. The timepiece, perhaps making an editorial comment about its surroundings, had stopped. The shopkeeper said that it was broken, but Norman bought it. He took it home, cleaned it, and got it running again. Sixty years later, the clock is still keeping time in the home of one of Norman's sons. "People seem to think that if a clock or a watch is no good you just throw it away. All it needed was a cleaning and an oiling."

Two weeks shy of his 98th birthday, Norman is treating himself much the same way. The tiny man with feathery white hair has kept his mind and body sharp by playing pool three times a day at a senior's care home in Brandon. He has a hearing aid for each ear and lays them out on the right and left sides of his glasses on his nightstand so that he can quickly grab and install them. He keeps his teeth under his pillow. These superficial signs of age are of little consequence when Norman produces some of the colourful birthday and anniversary cards that he made for the other residents. He made them while sitting in front of the care home's computer, pecking at the keys and moving the "squares" (what Bill Gates would call Windows).

Norman Chapman was born in 1900, and in 1998 he seemed to be a good bet to outlast the 20th century. His father, Thomas Chapman, was born near Bath, England, in 1850 — just six years after Louis Riel's birth — and moved to Canada the year that it became a nation. Thomas left Winnipeg to start a homestead southwest of Brandon, the same one where Norman was born and where he lived and farmed until 1983, when he moved into the care home.

His whole life, Norman has been a witness to the many ways in which technology has changed the work and home lives of people on the Prairies. His earliest memory is of himself, just three years old, standing beside his older brother by the banks of the Assiniboine River. "I can remember him firing the

166

shotgun to call the ferryman to come and get us." This must have been 1903, he says, because that brother died the following year.

The first car that young Norman ever laid eyes on was an Oldsmobile Runabout. "A man passed by our school one day, and myself and another boy ran out and stood on the back axle and rode it down the road. That was my first car ride."

Norman remembers when he considered four horses pulling a cart and plow a major improvement over the walking plow that his father had used. Now his son has an eight-wheeled John Deere. Norman talks in wonder of computerized combines and his son's solar-powered water pump. "It isn't the manual labour that it used to be. It's more mental now. They've got to use their head."

Norman's small room contains several photos and paintings of horses. A five-year-old newspaper clipping shows him seated upon his horse, a brown stallion on his son's farm. "In another week and a half, I'll be 98," Norman says. "And I'm planning to ride that fellow." (*In October 2003, Norman Chapman celebrated his 103rd birthday with his family.*)

> "My God, why would I ever leave this?"
> — *Gull Lake, Saskatchewan, farmer Vern Small*
>   *speaking about the Prairies in 1937*

Afterword

One final bit of advice, one that I can't claim as my own. It comes from Darlene Hay, the artist whom you met in chapter 3. It applies equally to the folks who live on the Prairies and to those who live somewhere else.

At some point, you'll find yourself driving down one of our long, straight highways, headed for some destination on the horizontal line that divides land and sky. Do yourself a favour. Pull over, turn the engine off, and get out of the car. Go for a walk through a field, down a country road, or along the main street of some town you've passed but never visited. Talk to people, or just listen to the distinct, gentle symphony of sounds.

Above all, get out of the car.

Sources

BOOKS

You Asked Us ... About Canada by Walter Stefaniuk, Doubleday Canada, Toronto, 1996; *Just Another Minute: More Glimpses of Our Great Canadian Heritage* by Marsha Boulton, Little, Brown and Company, Toronto, 1997; *The Canuck Book* by Ian Walker and Keith Bellows, General Publishing, Don Mills, ON, 1978; *Canada Firsts* by Ralph Nader, Nadia Milleron, and Duff Conacher, McClelland and Stewart, Toronto, 1992; *Colombo's Canadian References* by John Robert Colombo, John Deyell Company, 1976; *The Book of Canadians* by Carlotta Hacker, Hurtig Publishers, Edmonton, 1983; *Canada* by Mark Lightbody, Dorinda Talbot, Jim DuFresne, and Tom Smallman, Lonely Planet Publications, Hawthorne, Victoria, Australia, 1997; *"I Never Say Anything Provocative"* by John G. Diefenbaker, Peter Martin Associates, Toronto, 1975; *Prairie Lives* by Lois Ross, Between the Lines, Toronto, 1985; *Flashback Canada* by J. Bradley Cruxton and W. Douglas Wilson, Oxford University Press, Toronto, 1978; *Next-Year Country* by Barry Broadfoot, McClelland and Stewart, Toronto, 1988; *In a Sea of Wind* by Yva Momatiuk and John Eastcott, Camden House Publishing, Camden East, ON, 1991; *Coots, Codgers and Curmudgeons* by Hal Sisson and Dwayne Rowe, Orca Book Publishers, Victoria, 1994; *The Canadian Style* by Raymond Reid, Fitzhenry and Whiteside, Don Mills, ON, 1973; *The Prairies* by Tanya Lloyd, Whitecap Books, Vancouver, 1997; *Western People* edited by Mary L. Gilchrist, Western Producer Prairie Books, Saskatoon, 1988; *Colombo's Book of Marvels* by John Robert Colombo, NC Press, Toronto, 1979; *Coyote Music and Other Humorous Tales of the Early West* by Grant MacEwan, Rocky Mountain Books, Calgary, 1993; *Once Upon a Tomb* by Nancy Millar, Fifth House, Calgary, 1997; *Inventing Canada* by Roy Mayer, Raincoast Books, Vancouver, 1997; *Plainspeaking* by Doris Hillis, Coteau Books, Regina, 1996; *Voices and Visions* by Doris Hillis, Coteau Books, Regina, 1985; *Prairie Journal* by Bob Phillips, Western Producer Prairie Books, Saskatoon, 1986; *Struggle and Splendor* by Eldon Anderson, Panorama Publications, Regina, 1996; *The Golden Age of the Canadian Cowboy* by Hugh A. Dempsey, Fifth House, Saskatoon, 1995; *What's in a Name* by E. T. Russell, Western Producer Prairie Books, Saskatoon, 1973; *Courting Saskatchewan* by David Carpenter, Greystone Books, Vancouver, 1996; *Salt of the Earth* by Heather Robertson, James Lorimer, Toronto, 1974; *But It's a Dry Cold!* by Elaine Wheaton, Fifth House, Calgary, 1998; *Come 'n' Get It* by Beulah Barss, Western Producer Prairie Books, Saskatoon, 1983;

The Pioneer Cook by Beulah Barss, Detselig Enterprises, Calgary, 1980; *Unnatural History: True Manitoba Mysteries* by Chris Rutkowski, Chameleon Publishers, Winnipeg, 1993; *The Western Producer's First Half Century* by Keith Dryden, Modern Press, Saskatoon, 1973; *Dafoe of The Free Press* by Murray Donnelly, Macmillan of Canada, Toronto, 1968; *Eye-Opener Bob* by Grant MacEwan, Institute of Applied Art, Edmonton, 1957; *Torch on the Prairies: A Portrait of Journalism in Manitoba, 1859-1988* edited by Marjorie Earl, The Nor'Westers, Winnipeg, 1988; *White Hoods: Canada's Ku Klux Klan* by Julian Sher, New Star Books, Vancouver, 1983: *The One-Room School in Canada* by Jean Cochrane, Fitzhenry and Whiteside, Markham, ON, 1981; *Nikka Yuko Centennial Garden* by Lynne Van Luven, Lethbridge and District Japanese Garden Society, Lethbridge, 1980; *A Chronicle of the Canadian West*, North-West Mounted Police Report for 1875, Historical Society of Alberta, Calgary, 1975; *Soups and Borschts from Hutterite, Amish, Mennonite, Dutch, Ukrainian and Russian Kitchens* by Samuel Hofer, Hofer Publishing, Red Deer, 1988; *Pioneer Kitchens: Our Heritage from Many Lands*, Southern Alberta Pioneers, Centax Books, Regina, 1995; *Guide to Western Canada* by Frederick Pratson, Globe Pequot Press, Chester, Connecticut, 1987; *Cold as a Bay Street Banker's Heart: The Ultimate Prairie Phrase Book* by Chris Thain, Western Producer Prairie Books, Saskatoon, 1987; *Prairie Sentinel* by Brock Silversides, Fifth House, Calgary, 1997; *Barns of Western Canada* by Bob Hainstock, Braemar Books, Victoria, 1985; *Midways, Judges, and Smooth-Tongued Fakirs* by David C. Jones, Western Producer Prairie Books, Saskatoon, 1983; *The Canadian Encyclopedia*, Hurtig Publishers, Edmonton, 1985; *Forceps, Fin and Feather* by Wilfred Abram Bigelow, D. W. Friesen and Sons, Altona, MB, 1969; *Harvest of Bread* by Grant MacEwan, Western Producer Prairie Books, Saskatoon, 1969; *The Folk Festival Book* by Steve Johnson, Turnstone Press, Winnipeg; *Extraordinary Tales from Manitoba History* by J. W. Chafe, McClelland and Stewart, Toronto, 1973; *Manitoba Montage* by Earl Johnson, Panther Publications, Winnipeg, 1985; *The Suicide Battalion* by James L. McWilliams and R. James Steel, Hurtig Publishers, Edmonton, 1978; *The Canada Trip* by Charles Gordon, McClelland and Stewart, Toronto, 1997; *Winter and Summer Excursions in Canada* by Catharine Laura Johnstone, Digby Long, London, UK, n.d.; *Religious Settlement on the Prairies* edited by Benjamin Smillie, NeWest Press, Edmonton, 1983; *The People* by Donald Ward, Fifth House, Saskatoon, 1995; *The Face-Pullers: Photography of Native Canadians* by Brock V. Silversides, Fifth House, Saskatoon, 1994; *Through Indian Eyes*, Reader's Digest Association (Canada), Montreal, 1996; *Riel: A Life of*

Revolution by Maggie Siggins, HarperCollins Publishers, Toronto, 1994; *Red Coats on the Prairies* by William Beahen and Stan Horrall, Centax Books, Regina, 1998; *Native Foods and Nutrition*, Health Canada, Ottawa, 1994; *Gwen's Favourite Recipes* by Gwen Duguid and Louise Newans, self-published, Manitoba, 1992; *Fort Chipewyan Traditional Cookery*, Fort Chipewyan Historical Society, 1994; *Eastern and Western Perspectives* edited by David Jay Bercuson and Phillip A. Buckner, University of Toronto Press, Toronto, 1978; *The Wild Frontier* by Pierre Berton, McClelland and Stewart, Toronto, 1978; *West to the Sea* by J. W. Grant MacEwan, McGraw-Hill, Toronto, 1968; *National Hockey League Official Guide and Record Book 1997-98*, National Hockey League, New York, 1998; *Ukrainian Daughters' Cookbook*, Ukrainian Women's Association of Canada, Daughters of Ukraine Branch, Regina, 1984; *Saskatchewan History along the Highway* by Bob Weber, Red Deer College Press, Red Deer, 1998; *Forging the Prairie West* by John Herd Thompson, Oxford University Press, Don Mills, ON, 1998; *Shakin' All Over: The Rock and Roll Years in Canada* edited by Peter Goddard and Philip Kamin, McGraw-Hill Ryerson, Toronto, 1989.

PERIODICALS
1998 Visitors' Guide, Fort Macleod, AB; the *Regina Free Press*; the *Leader-Post* (Regina); the *Edmonton Journal*; the *Calgary Herald*; the *Toronto Star*; the *Winnipeg Free Press*; the *Globe and Mail*; *Maclean's*, February 13, 1995; the *Prairie Dog* (Regina); "Profile of Canada's Aboriginal Population, 1991," Statistics Canada, Ottawa, 1995; "Control and Sale of Alcoholic Beverages in Canada (1995-1996)," Statistics Canada, Ottawa, 1998; "Canadians on the Move" by Bali Ram, Y. Edward Shin, and Michel Poliot, *Focus on Canada*, Statistics Canada, Ottawa, 1994; "Religions in Canada," Statistics Canada, Ottawa, 1993; "Home Language and Mother Tongue," Statistics Canada, Ottawa, 1993; "Who Gives to Charity?" by Jeffrey Frank and Stephen Mihorean, *Canadian Social Trends 43*, Statistics Canada, winter 1996; "Language and Culture of the Métis People" by Josée Normand, Canadian Social Trends 43, Statistics Canada, Ottawa, winter 1996; 1996 Census, Statistics Canada, Ottawa, 1996; *The Thin Red Line* by Red Coat Trail Historical Association, Eastend, SK; *Credit Union Way*, Credit Union Central of Saskatchewan, Regina, 1998; *Buffalo Trails and Tales*, Métis Resource Centre, Winnipeg.

INTERVIEWS

Darlene Hay, Lorne and Norma Hunter, Scott Bonnor, Reverend Stan Cuthand, Marie Hoffman, Kent Woods, Dick and Tom Heapy, Harvey English, George and Elias Hofer, Dr. Paul Bookhalter, Rolande Rheault, Mary Perron, Fred Free, Larry Gnius, Jeff Watson, Toini Pettersson, Norm Suenm, Don Dempson, Bryn Thiessen, Mabel Geary, Del Fraser, Morris Elfenbaum, Lorraine Freeman, Jean Bates, Adam Becker, Kate McWhir, Frank Sisson, Robin Burwash, Gordon Pittman, Al Duerr, Andrew Yskes, Christina Kaulbach-Stosuy, Steve Tsongas, and Norman (Mr. 20th Century) Chapman.

OTHER

Head-Smashed-In Buffalo Jump Interpretive Centre; Saskatchewan Sports Hall of Fame; Alberta Sports Hall of Fame and Museum; Manitoba Sports Hall of Fame and Museum; Saskatchewan Science Centre; Alberta, Saskatchewan, and Manitoba provincial tourism offices; Saskatoon and Regina city clerks' offices; Métis Resource Centre, Winnipeg.

PERMISSIONS

The passage from *Flashback Canada* © J. Bradley Cruxton and W. Douglas Wilson (Oxford University Press, 1978), excerpted on page 31, is reproduced by permission of Oxford University Press Canada.

The passage from *The Canada Trip* by Charles Gibson (McCelland and Stewart, 1997), excerpted on page 167, is used by permission, McClelland and Stewart, Inc. The Canadian Publishers.

Passages from *Extraordinary Tales from Manitoba History* by J. W. Chafe (Manitoba Historical Society, 1973), excerpted on pages 151 and elsewhere, are reproduced by permission of the Manitoba Historical Society.

Passages from *Voices and Visions* by Doris Hillis (1985), published by Coteau Books, excerpted on page 144, are used with permission of the publisher.

Passages from *Prairie Lives* by Lois Ross (Between the Lines Press, 1985), excerpted on pages 70, 78 and 79, are reproduced by permission of the publisher.

Passages from *The Canadian Style* © by Raymond Ried, published by Fitzhenry and Whiteside, Markham, Ontario, excerpted on page 164, are reprinted with permission of the publisher.

Various selections excerpted from *Coyote Music and Other Humorous Tales of the Early West* by Grant MacEwan (Rocky Mountain Books, 1993) are reproduced by permission of the publisher.

The passages from *Eye-Opener Bob* by Grant MacEwan, excerpted on page 139, is reproduced with the kind permission of Mr. MacEwan.

The passage from *Forceps, Fin and Feather* by Wilfred Abram Bigelow (D. W. Friesen, 1969), is reproduced by permission of Friesens.